AF431412

"Our ancestors have sinned. Now they are gone, but we continue to suffer the punishment that they deserved."

Copyright © 2019 Reuben Laurore

All rights reserved.

ISBN: 979-8-60-648172-9

Before
Shackles & Chains

By: Reuben Laurore

Illustrations by Tony Foti

DEDICATION

To my sons, I want you to always remember that your lineage is glorious. You are of Haitian descent, a people who are abundant in spirituality and strength, a people who are the bones of humanity, and a people who broke the chains of bondage off of the world. Trace back down the line of your fathers and remember you are also of a holy bloodline. My father, his father, his fore fathers before him, and I are all descendants of the Sons of God. Live by the truths that I have taught you and share them. I have started the work I have been called to do, continue this work after me and teach your sons to do the same. You all have continuously made me proud and I take great pride in being called your father.

To my people, all who are descendants of the Trans-Atlantic Slave Trade, though you have suffered throughout history, you are beyond rich. The lies you have been taught have blinded you temporarily, but it will never change the truth of who you are; nor will it change your destiny. You are a special people of a royal divine line. This truth is currently not common knowledge; however, it soon will be. I dedicate this book to you in hope that it will awaken the spirit of brotherhood, sisterhood, and unity within you. We share one common enemy, it is not each other, but the world. All nations have mutually enslaved, oppressed, and mocked us. This is how it has been for our ancestors in the past, and it is still the case for us today. For the sake of our God's name, we have survived up to this point. We are His glory, in the near future we will finally awake from our slumber and be restored to our proper place in this world. Not a single member of our people, dead or alive, will ever be lost. In fact, all of us will rise on that day. May peace be with you and may you come to remember who you truly are.

CONTENTS

"A people without the knowledge of their past history, origin, and culture is like a tree without roots." Marcus Garvey

-1-
THE IDENTITY CRISIS

Ever since I was a young boy, the only history of myself that I have ever known was slavery and captivity. In school we were taught that our history ran back as much as 400-500 years. Growing up, I have never questioned this, neither have my family members or friends. With full trust and confidence in an education system supposedly formulated by noble men, my parents sent me to school without any doubt about what I was actually learning. Nonetheless, we were being taught by the nation that currently houses prisoners of war, the nation partially responsible for the enslavement of my people and the lies of my origin. It is a story that is accepted generation after generation, a story that says my beginning starts with bondage. Even in media and entertainment, my people are continuously shown in roles of servitude. Every year during black history month, we are reminded that we were slaves and nothing more. Simply take time and really think about what that does to someone psychologically.

I've asked several African American friends of mine who they were prior to slavery and most have said they didn't know nor had they really thought about it. Other than a general lack of knowledge, there were some that said Cherokee, Native American, or just African. I have asked several of my Jamaican friends who they were prior to being known as Jamaicans. All of them responded with, "slaves." I then asked who they were prior to slavery, most of their responses were they did not know, others said some type of African. Being of Haitian descent, my answer to this question was always West African. I have asked several of my Haitian friends and family members who they were prior to being known as Haitian people. All of their responses included slavery. I proceeded to ask what they were prior to slavery. Most said African, some said they didn't know, some said Nigerian, and some said Congolese. I wanted to delve a little deeper into this particular subject. I decided to conduct my own survey, in which I asked 100 random non-African black people who they were or where they specifically came from prior to slavery. The results were staggering. Majority of people, being 86 percent, said they do not know, four percent said Egypt, two percent said Ghana, and two percent said Nigeria. The lesser percentage of the people I asked gave answers such as Moors, Cherokee, German, Ethiopian, Hebrew, kings and queens. Everyone who I asked hesitated before thinking of an answer, and all who actually named a location were uncertain. Can the same be said for anyone else? Is there another nation of people whose history goes in countless different directions? Is there a group of people on this planet who have no idea who they are or where they came from?

Go to the land of China, to the Chinese man, and inquire about his history. He can confidently tell you that his people have roughly over 3000 years of civilization. He can continue on by explaining that his native tongue is Chinese, and how most of Chinese history can be divided up into a series of dynasties, from the start of the Xia dynasty in 2205 BCE to the end of the Qing dynasty in 1912 CE. A time period when rich culture was born, unique names thought up, beautiful music orchestrated, martial arts mastered, unique architecture constructed, sophisticated engineering developed, and so much more was being accomplished. One of those great accomplishments being the Great Wall of China, which was built roughly around 220 BC. A wall so vast that it can be seen from space and has become one of the 7 Wonders of the World. Another accomplishment being the invention of paper by Cai Lun around 105 CE. Around 250 CE, Buddhism, one of the three main religions of China, was introduced. A religion appreciated and practiced all around the world today. During the Tang Dynasty, the first use of wood block printing took place, roughly around 868 CE. The Song Dynasty can be proud to say that during that period, gunpowder was also invented around 1044 CE; it was first used for fireworks. Later on, around 1088 CE, the magnetic compass was invented. The Chinese man can go to lengths telling you about his story and yet, he is not alone.

Go to land of Mexico, to the Mexican man, and inquire about his history. He can tell you that the Mexicans are descendants of the ancient Aztec people. An incredible people who were highly skilled engineers that built the marvelous city Tenochtitlan. Among other things, they were the first to implement universal compulsory education. They had a number system, a calendar, great knowledge of medicine, and a rich tradition of poetry. The Aztec civilization flourished between 1350 CE-1522 CE. The Mexican man can tell you his ancestor's native language was Nahuatl, prior to his current tongue, Spanish. One of the many great accomplishments of the Aztecs was their ability to create artificial islands called chinampas. The chinampas were a highly productive form of cultivation. Another impressive accomplishment was how far ahead they were with herbalism. They had a codex, the Badianus Manuscript, which explains how you can use about 200 trees and plants to cure ailments. Lastly, one of the most marvelous monuments of the Aztecs are the temples and pyramids that were built with such precision and accuracy. Temples and pyramids were built in order to honor and house their deities. I truly appreciate the richness of their architecture. Prior to being colonized by the Spanish in the 16th century, Mexico covers a period of more than three millennia. One of the great accomplishments of the Mexican people include the color television, invented by Guillermo Gonzalez Camarena on September 15, 1942. A few more Mexican inventions include the windmill, magnetic brakes, the wrench, and a reversible motor. This was all done by Victor Ochoa. Maria Gonzalez patented her processes to diagnose invasive amebiasis, a parasitic disease that kills over 100,000 people each year. There is much more that the Mexicans have offered the world throughout their history.

Go to the land of Italy, to the Italian man, and

inquire about his history. He can tell you that he is a descendant of the formidable Roman Empire. An empire that was one of the most powerful and influential civilizations in world history, lasting over 1000 years. Rome began around 753 BC and grew to rule much of Europe, Western Asia, and Northern Africa. Some extraordinary achievements of Rome include the construction of paved roads, drains, aqueducts, amphitheaters, theaters, stadiums, public spas, the colosseum, Roman calendar, hydraulics, law, governance, and the Roman alphabet, which forms the core of the English language. The Roman Empire was truly an advanced empire and is still impactful on the world today. Now fast forward to the fall of the Roman Empire, 476 AD, to the Iron Age, 900 BC, and the birth of the Italians. After the fall of Rome, many Romans migrated to Italy. A beautiful country which comprises some of the most varied scenic landscapes on earth. Its inhabitants appreciate a high standard of living and a highly developed culture. Italy has a span of history of over 3000 years, and is home to one of the world's most influential centers of religion, literature, visual arts, music, philosophy, sciences, and culinary arts. Some inventions by the Italians include the newspaper, telephone, jeans, Jacuzzi, radio, batteries, piano, banks, espresso machine, and plenty more.

Lastly, go and journey down to Africa, the mother land. Go to the land of Ethiopia, to the Ethiopian man, and inquire about his history. He can boast about having arguably one of the oldest and most colorful histories of any African kingdom. A kingdom that was never occupied by a European power. Founded around 980 BC, for thousands of years people have lived in Ethiopia. However, in the first century AD, Ethiopia's rise truly begins. By 100 AD a kingdom called the Axum was born. Born of the Hebrew King Solomon and the Ethiopian Queen Sheba. Two powerful rulers had a son named Menelik, who goes to Ethiopia and establishes the royal dynasty. The Axum kingdom became a regional trading power and lasted for over a millennium. The Ethiopian man can tell you that Ethiopia's most famous residents was roughly 3.2 million years ago. Some of the oldest skeletons discovered were found in this rich land. He can also tell you that the Omo valley is one of the most diverse tribal places in Africa. Some of the astounding accomplishments of the Ethiopians are the construction of the Sofomar cave, the lion of Judah monument, Lalibela, being among the earliest coffee growers, the invention of computer chips that communicate with pulses of light vs electrical signals, the production of sorghum, and the launching of the world's first satellite radio system. Large volume books can be written about the Ethiopian man's history.

Let us conclude this chapter by discussing the point I am making. If you go and ask the Dogon, Moorish, Nigerian, Kenyan, Tanzanian, Ugandan, Egyptian, Ghanaian, Congolese, Cameroonian, Liberian, Japanese, Korean, Filipino, Indian, Taiwanese, Pakistani, Syrian, Saudi Arabian, Thais, Mongolian, Swedish, Greek, Irish, German, Russian, French, Spaniard, Ukrainian, Khazar (European Jews), Saponi, Lenape, Tutelo, Seneca, Cherokee, or the Mayan man of his story, he can give you a confident, proud history lesson. Ask the nations about their names and the meaning of them. Who out of all the nations in the world would be unable to give you an answer? I know of only one, the descendants of the lost nation that was captured by many African countries, then sold to Europeans, Asians, and Arabs as prisoners of war. Later to be enslaved in Africa, the Americas, Europe, Asia and all around the world. Go and ask non- African black people the same exact questions as the ones previously asked in the beginning of his chapter. I can say with 1000 percent certainty that either their dubious answers will differ from one another or they more than likely will genuinely not know. Ask them to trace back their lineage. Ask any one of the children of this lost nation what their names were prior to the last names that were branded onto them during slavery, foreign names that they currently carry and pass down to their children's children. Majority of them cannot proudly or confidently provide you with an answer. Throughout time all around the world, the notion of names, as it is directly connected to identity, has always been considerably important. Names are not just letters that sound pleasant, they are carefully chosen and created with deep meaning and purpose. A name contains power and it propels people to move towards greatness. The vibration in names can invoke something deep within you and draw out energy and power. Names can be a gift or a curse, bringing about good fortune or bad. Names shape who we are, but most importantly they tell a story. They tell a unique story of nations, individuals and generations they belong to. It links us to our roots, our ancestors and origin. The last names of black people (specifically the descendants of the Trans-Atlantic Slave trade) tell a story of slavery and identifies current day prisoners of war. You have a nation of people who know no true home land to call their own, who do not know their native tongue, who are entirely disconnected from their roots, who do not know where they specifically came from, who do not know their original names, or anything about themselves. Is this not by definition an identity crisis? A severe one, I might add. Who were the black slaves? What country did they come from? Who are their ancestors? Why were they stripped of everything known about them? Why did African nations collaborate with each other and with Europeans, Asians and Arabs to destroy them? Why is their history never spoken about or taught in schools? What is their true identity? Read on as the upcoming chapters dig deep into this crisis to discover and surface the biggest kept secret of all time.

"The original design is filled with more soul and life than the copy. Accepted by the rays of the sun are the children of nature."

-2-

THE HYBRIDS

I've often wondered about the explanation given by scientist pertaining to the diversity of people within the human race. Among human beings, there is the so called "black", red, yellow, and white man. Although we humans share similarities, the differences between the races are so drastic that we seem alien to one another. Is it possible that through migration, climate change, and years of evolution, one can go from having dark brown skin, hair, and eyes to having white skin, blue eyes, and blonde hair? I do not believe it so. To go from one extreme to the other, or one end of the spectrum to the opposite end, just doesn't exactly add up. To credit these drastic changes to location and weather is criminal to the truth. Such a bold claim deserves heavy research on an important topic such as the origins of the human race.

According to National Geographic studies, scientists agree that everyone alive today can trace their ancestry back to Africa—the place referred to as the Motherland. Their theory is that humans ventured out of Africa roughly 60,000 years ago, leaving behind genetic footprints that are visible today. The migration of these early humans is what led the small group of Africans to occupy the farthest ends of the earth. They have concluded that our species is an African one and that Africa is where we have spent most of our time on earth. Based on this study, it is safe to say that the original humans on earth are melanated people; therefore, the so-called black man and black woman are the parents of humanity. If the original people of the earth are still alive today, who or what are the people walking side by side with them? Being that so-called black people are the mother and father of all races, how did such dominate genes change so drastically?

An international team of researchers led by Damian Labuda, of the Department of Pediatrics at the University of Montreal, conducted a study on genetic research. What they found is that some of the X chromosome originates from Neanderthals and is found solely in non-African people. This research was published in the issue of Molecular Biology and Evolution. Dr. Labuda and his team identified a piece of DNA called a haplotype that was foreign to human DNA. When the Neanderthal genome was sequenced in 2010, they compared 6000 chromosomes from all parts of the world to the Neanderthal haplotype. The Neanderthal sequence was present in all people across all continents except for Africa. Dr. David Reich, a Harvard Medical School geneticist, is one of the principal researchers in the Neanderthal genome project and agrees with these findings.

Another study was done on the origins of blue eyes and blonde hair. The study found that only two percent of the world's population are natural blondes. According to a team of researchers from Copenhagen University, the blue eyes and blonde hair gene, called OCA2, arose as recently as 6,000-10,000 years ago. This research was published in the journal, Human Genetics. Now, you have Africans who are earth's original people that have 100 percent human DNA, then you have non-African people who are earth's foreigners that have two percent or more Neanderthal (non-human) DNA. The offspring of a reproductive cross between genetically dissimilar individuals of different species, sub-species, or the offspring of two different things resulting in something that has a little bit of both is by definition a hybrid. The number one piece of evidence of this fact lies in the sun, which carries life energy in its rays to our planet. It identifies both groups of people as its light embraces the children of the sun by energizing them, but rejects the children nonnative to earth by burning them. The sun and earth work together in harmony to try and eliminate what does not belong in the planet, in the same way the human body tries to rid itself of anything foreign that enters it. Scientist theorize that these mutations begin with early humans mating with Neanderthals. I strongly disagree with this theory. Our ancient ancestors—who were far more superior than we are technologically, mathematically, astrologically, spiritually, and in every regard—have a different story than scientists do today.

Many ancient civilizations speak of advanced beings from other worlds in distant solar systems coming to earth and genetically modifying certain groups of humans to raise, operate through, and carry out their agenda. Several civilizations also speak of advanced beings from other universes or dimensions that came to earth and implanted their DNA in certain races of humans, parenting who they considered or selected to be their chosen people. Certain nations were the representation of their god/gods on earth. This has been a mutual story worldwide; these advanced visitors of the past seem to all have a personal agenda that involved the human race. There has also been claims that alien beings have genetically modified some animals, creating unoriginal creatures (through mixing DNA of different creatures) that ended up not being harmonious with nature. An example of such a creature are the dinosaurs. This was a failed project due to the dinosaur's nature causing them to devour everything on earth. This issue was so severe it is said that alien beings had to intervene and destroy the dinosaurs before they destroyed the human project. The beings that visited us in our distant past still visit us today. The difference only being that today we refer to them as aliens, whereas back then they were referred to as gods. I would like to bring attention to the bold claims of Canada's former minister of National Defense, Paul Hellyer. In 2013 at the Citizen Hearing on Disclosure in Washington D.C., Paul Hellyer encouraged world powers to reveal information on UFOs and the presence of aliens to the public. Paul Hellyer testified that alien beings are living among us and that at least two of them are working with the U.S. government. In fact, he states that different alien species are working hand-in-hand with different governments all around the world. He goes on to say that there are currently 80 known species of aliens and they all have their own agenda. Here are a few statements made by Paul Hellyer. "The whole cosmos is a unity, and it affects not just us, but other people in the cosmos, they're very much afraid that we might be stupid enough to start using atomic weapons again. This would be bad for us and for them too." Another statement explains, "Some of the aliens hail from the Zeta Reticuli, the Pleiades, Orion, Andromeda, and Altair star systems and may have different agendas." Here, Paul is explaining the different planets and solar systems these beings come from. He continues on by stating, "A shadowy cabal compromised of the Council on Foreign Relations, the Bilderbergers, The Trilateral Commission, the international banking cartel, the oil cartel, members of various intelligence organizations, and select members of the military junta control world affairs and are scheming to create one world government." Again, this isn't new knowledge, alien beings have been visiting earth and living among us since the ancient world, possibly before humans walked the earth. This is still the case today. It is said that these beings are dwelling underground, deep within mountains and deep within our oceans. Thousands of eye witness accounts of UFO/alien sightings are documented in the U.S. alone, and thousands upon thousands are documented around the world. Another difference between then and now is that the alien beings directly interacted with entire nations publicly, versus today where it seems alien beings privately interact with the elite or government. Earth has been an experimental ground for these other worldly beings since the beginning of time. Let us explore a few ancient civilization stories of creation and their god's involvement with mankind.

The Dogon people of Africa believed in a creator god named Amma. Amma created everything out of a pot of clay. Over a course of time, he created a lesser god named Nommo. Nommo was said to be an inhabitant of a world circling the star Sirius. Nommo was responsible for teaching mankind the sacred revelations that give order to the world. The first revelation was the laws of nature, the second was order, and the third was granary and the drum.

The Mayan people of Central America believed in the beginning two gods created everything. These gods would create simply by speaking everything into existence. These gods created the earth and everything in it. Humans were created last after several failed attempts and experimentation. These Mayan gods destroyed and recreated humans about three different times until they finally got it right and the creation of the human race was a success. After humans multiplied and many years passed by, a god named Kukuklan came down and taught the Mayans everything they knew. He taught them how to read, write, live, etc. He is said to be from Orion star system.

The Sumerian people of Mesopotamia believed in the creator god An. An was the chief god of gods and created the Annunaki, the gods of the Sumerians. The Annunaki came from a planet called Nibiru. They visited earth to mine gold for their planet's atmosphere. The work was burdensome so they decided to create humans to perform the work for them. The first set of humans were created in the image and likeness of the gods, from the blood and body of a god that was put to death. These humans were unable to reproduce so they were genetically modified by the Annunaki. The first humans created were unsuccessful and had to be modified and recreated roughly six times. The seventh time the gods finally were successful by implanting their DNA within the humans.

Finally, you have the Hebrew people; who are also known as Israelites. They believe in one Supreme God who is nameless but holds the tittle King of Kings. He goes by "I AM that I AM". He is the Creator and Source of all creation, the All in all. The Hebrew people, believe He created humans ("black" people) in His image and likeness. Man-kind (all non-Africans) were later on created in the image and likeness of humans and other beings. However, the Hebrew's bloodline was set apart from humanity because they were specifically chosen by God. They also believe that they are the carnal embodiment/vessels of His Spirit making them His children. After their God created His earthly offspring, He chose them to be His representatives that were to rule and have dominion over earth. He gave them His laws and statutes, taught them how to build their society, fathered them, and raised them up as His own. They today are known as God's chosen People.

A Hebrew patriarch named Enoch was said to be taken into outer space by beings from the same dimension of this God. He was deemed righteous by God and was invited to live in this God's planet. In Enoch's book, he documented the presence of watchers/guardians of the earth that came down and taught humans all sort of forbidden knowledge. He also stated that they implanted their DNA into the human race which gave birth to man-kind/hybrids not harmonious to the planet, one race of hybrids being the giants. Their offspring would do nothing but evil deeds while terrorizing the planet. These watchers continued working with these hybrids who became their chosen people to fulfill their personal agenda.

Many people have theorized that some creatures bare the mark of alien intervention, such as the octopus—a creature revered as sacred in the ancient world. The octopus is a mysterious creature not fully understood and very alien to all other creatures on the planet. Having three hearts and nine brains, the octopus has over 50,000 genes in comparison to humans, who only have roughly 25,000. However, this isn't the only factor that makes these extraordinary creatures alien like. They are able to shape shift, camouflage, manipulate its environment, and above all edit its DNA. Several people believe that if an animal species was to evolve and become the superior creatures on the planet, it would indeed be the octopus.

Science, religion, and legend all have a mutual agreement here. Something has continuously intervened with humans and diversified the human race causing a big change in the original agenda/design. The intervention of these beings has caused great regression or quick technological advances among the humans. These interventions have thrown off the balance of the world, eliminating perfect harmony and order. Not all genetically modified foods or hybrid animals are of the same scientist, nor were they born out of the same lab. In the same way, not all people are of the same origin or of the same God/gods. Similar to the liger, wholphins, beefalo, zebroids, grolar bear, pigs, dogs, cats, mules, mosquitos, hornets, certain fruits, and vegetables. Humans, are too, subject to genetic modification. Recently scientists have created the first successful human-animal-hybrid according to National Geographic. This new creation is accredited to its creator, whoever the scientist may be. In the same way, the Hebrew people are the glory of their God. Their history says that they are a race of gods, part god and part man. They are gods living in flesh. These aliens, so to speak, all had their own agenda in their tampering with humans. What was the God of the Hebrews agenda?

"For so sworn good or evil an oath may not be broken and it shall pursue oath keeper and oath breaker to the world's end." J.R. R Tolkien

THE COVENANT

Before getting into who the Hebrew people are, we must first learn of their origin. Their history can be found in the Torah or the Bible. I will reference these books while telling their story. At some point in time, the God of the Hebrews came into this universe from another dimension. He desired to have offspring for purposes known to Himself. He traveled throughout the universe, chose a spot in space, and created our solar system and its planets. Earth, a marvel in itself, a beautiful and habitable planet, was found fitting to plant His Seed. In the book of Genesis (first book of the Hebrews history book) chapter 1 verse 26, it reads: "Then God said, let Us make man in Our image, after Our likeness. And let them rule over the fish of the sea and the birds of the sky, over the wild animals and over the whole earth, and over all creatures that move along the ground." Here we see that the God of the Hebrews has created His first earthly son named Adam. He has bestowed upon him authority to rule over the entire planet. In the Quran, God commands all of His angels after creating Adam, to bow down in reverence to him.

Although Adam was the first earthly son of God, there were other humans living on the planet. Adam was not the first person to live on the earth, contrary to popular belief. Fast forwarding a little, a woman was created for Adam and given to him; the woman's name was Eve. Eve disobeyed God after being seduced by a "serpent" (deceitful person). She committed adultery with this deceiver resulting in both participants of this forbidden act, to be cursed by God. God stated that there would be animosity between the offspring of the serpent and the future offspring of Eve. Eve ended up pregnant and had a son named Cain. Cain was the son of the deceitful one. After the birth of Cain, Adam and Eve later on had a son named Abel. These two half-brothers were the first two offspring Eve. One being born of infidelity, according to the gospel of Philip. Evidence of Cain's lineage being of the serpent is stated in the book of 1 John chapter 3 verse 12: "Do not be like Cain, who belonged to the evil one and murdered his brother. And why did he murder him? Because his own actions were evil and his brothers were righteous." Cain, out of jealousy, ended up killing his younger half-brother and getting banished out of their domain. Abel found favor with God while Cain did not. While Cain was roaming the earth, their book mentions him discovering cities and establishments prior to Adam and Eve having another child, proving there were people living on the planet outside of Adam's lineage. This is evident in Genesis 4:14 where Cain says to the God of the Hebrews, "You have banished me from the land and your presence; you have made me a homeless wanderer on earth. Anyone who finds me will kill me." Cain is fully aware that there are other people living on the earth and is terrified to leave his land because he is confident that he would be killed if he does. It goes on to say that when Cain left the land, he ended up getting married. Genesis chapter 4:17 reads, "Cain made love to his wife, and she became pregnant and gave birth to Enoch…" Upon being exiled, Cain finds a wife who is not of the offspring of Adam and Eve and starts a family with her. In fact, when more Hebrew men descended from Adam, they begin intermarrying outside of their race. Genesis 6:2 says, "The sons of God saw that the daughters of men were beautiful. And they took as their wives any they chose." I am referencing these events to bring attention to the fact that at that time there existed separate bloodlines and nations. There was Adams bloodline (sons of God), the line of humans (Africans), man-kind (non-Africans), the line of the giants (hybrids), and more. Another example is when the God of the Hebrews was angered by Eve being seduced by the "serpent," whom she committed fornication with. As stated earlier, this act resulted in them both being cursed. Genesis 3:14-15 reads, "Then the LORD God said to the serpent, because you have done this, you are cursed above all animals, domestic and wild. On your belly you will move and dust you will eat all the days of your life. And I will put hostility between you and the woman, and between your offspring and her offspring; he will crush your head, and you will bruise his heel." This verse describes eternal enmity between two lines of people (sons of Gods vs man-kind), similar to the eternal hatred between lions and hyenas. The "serpent" being the father of one line and Adam being the father of the other. I put serpent in quotations because the book is not referring to a snake. There is not a group of people who have enmity with serpents or hostility with rattle snakes. This chapter refers to two future nations who will not be able to live side by side. One nation will first oppress the other nation and later on the oppressed nation will destroy the nation of their oppressors.

Adams offspring begin to multiply and many patriarchs of Adam found favor with the God of the Hebrews. I want to also make clear that not all of Adams descendants are sons and daughters of God and not all of Adams descendants are Hebrew. It is like a king having a son by his queen and having a son by one of his concubines. Both sons are technically of royal bloodline; however, the son of the queen's womb has true right to the throne. It is his birthright. The son of the concubine's womb has no claim at all; he is a bastard and nothing more. In this example you can better understand that a certain bloodline of Adam was chosen and declared children of God, hence making them rightful heirs of everything their heavenly Father owns. After time has passed, a man named Abraham was born who found favor with the God of the Hebrews and became very close with God. The God of the Hebrews favored him so much that He decided that He would choose one of Abraham's sons to become the father of the race of His chosen children. Abraham had a son named Ishmael and a son named Isaac. It was through Isaac that the everlasting covenant would be made between the Hebrews and their God. In Romans 9:4, the scripture reads: "They of Israel, chosen to be God's adopted children. God revealed His glory to them. He made covenants with them and gave them His law. He gave them the privilege of worshiping Him and receiving His promises."

Isaac, the son of Abraham, grew up and got married. He had two sons named Esau and Jacob. Jacob was the chosen vessel whom God loved, while Esau was hated by Him for reasons unknown. Jacob would go on to become known as Israel, the one who will give birth to the Hebrew nation. Jacob grew up and had several wives. His wives gave birth to 12 sons who became known as the 12 Tribes of Israel. His sons' names were Reuben, Simeon, Levi, Judah, Dan, Naphtali, Gad, Asher, Issachar, Zebulun, Joseph, and Benjamin. These 12 princes of God multiplied into individual tribes and were together known as the Israelites. Twelve nations united under their heavenly Father, called Israel.

As time went on and the Hebrews multiplied in North East Africa, they migrated into Egypt during the time of a great famine. Joseph, one of Jacob's sons, gained a high position of power in Egypt. The Pharaoh and Joseph became close friends which resulted in the Pharaoh providing the Hebrews with land in Egypt and the start of a strong relationship between respected neighbors. The Hebrews began to increase in number extremely quick. After Joseph and the Pharaoh died, the future Pharaoh felt no bond between the Hebrews and no reason to maintain a relationship with them. He also feared that at the rate they were multiplying, they would eventually grow into a powerful nation, fight them together with their enemies, and leave or over throw them. In the book of Exodus 1:8- 17, it reads: "Now a new pharaoh arose over Egypt, who did not know Joseph. He said to his people. Look the sons of

Israel are more and mightier than us. Come let us deal wisely with them or else they will multiply and in the event of war, they will also join themselves to those who hate us, fight against us, and leave the country. So, the Egyptians enslaved the Hebrews and put them to work. They put slave masters over them to press them with forced labor, and they built Pithom and Rameses as store cities for Pharaoh. However, the more they were oppressed, the more they multiplied and spread; so the Egyptians came to dread the Israelites and worked them ruthlessly. They made their lives miserable. The Egyptians were cruel to them and forced difficult work with harsh labor in brick and mortar and with all kinds of work in the fields; in all their harsh labor the Egyptians worked them ruthlessly. The Pharaoh said to the Hebrew midwives, whose names were Shiphrah and Puah. When you help the Hebrew women as they give birth, watch as they deliver. If the baby is a boy, kill him; if it is a girl, let her live. The midwives however feared God and did not do what Pharaoh commanded them, they let the boys live."

The Egyptians went on and enslaved the Hebrews for roughly 200 of the 430 years they spent living in Egypt. Towards the end of the 300-year mark, a leader was born of the Hebrews named Moses, who later on led their revolution. Moses specifically descended from the tribe of Levi, which was the priesthood tribe of the 12 tribes. Moses was adopted into the royal family of Egypt during the crisis when Hebrew male babies were being killed. He grew up under the impression that he was Egyptian, nevertheless he later found out the truth of who he was. After he learned he was Hebrew, he dreaded the way the Egyptians treated his people. One day there was an incident where Moses killed a slave master for persecuting and abusing one of his people. Out of fear of Egyptian law, which would have cost him his life, he fled the country. Through the desert, he journeyed to a foreign land called Midian, where he met his wife and started a family. This was where he also, for the first time, met the God of the Hebrews, specifically on a mountain called Mount Horeb.

Moses and God communicated directly with each other for a while and Moses was sent back to Egypt to deliver the Hebrews out of captivity and bring them to a mountain called Mount Sinai. This was where their God would meet His children. Moses did exactly that, he went back to one of the world's most powerful empires and worked great wonders to deliver his people out of Egypt. He accomplished this mission with ease by utilizing unmatched occult power and military expertise. Moses dealt with the Egyptians so violently through the sacred arts that the God of the Hebrews taught him, that the Egyptians gave them reparations and gold as they danced out of Egypt's borders. In fact, many Egyptians renounced their gods and left their home land to accompany the sons and daughters of God. It was impossible for them to live their previous lives after what their eyes had witnessed, or to ever forget the devastation Moses brought upon their country and people. Through the desert, they journeyed until they based themselves at the feet of Mount Sinai. This is where the covenant would be made, where God would meet His children and a nation would officially be established. Moses, who was now the mediator between the Hebrews and their God, went up the mountain to hear the terms of their heavenly Father. This is because when God spoke, the

Hebrews feared hearing His voice directly as it thundered through their souls. They couldn't handle the power that radiated from the vibrations of His voice; it caused them to be filled with horror. Deuteronomy 20:19 says, "And they said to Moses, you speak to us and we will listen. But don't let God speak to us directly, or we will die."

After the meeting, Moses came back down the mountain with laws (Ten Commandments) written by the hands of God, statutes, terms, and everything that was a part of the agreement. He carefully went over the terms which basically stated that if they keep their end of the covenant they would be blessed beyond measure; however, if they were to violate the covenant they would be cursed for a very long period of time. The Hebrews all together agreed to enter a sacred covenant with this God they have come to personally know. In their history book, the following chapter goes into further detail of the covenant's terms. In Deuteronomy 28:1-14, it reads: "If you faithfully obey the LORD your God and carefully follow all of His commandments that I am giving you today, the LORD your God will set you high above all the nations of the world. You will experience all these blessings if you obey the LORD your God. You will be blessed in the city and blessed in the country. Your children and your crops will be blessed. The offspring of your herds and flocks will be blessed. Your fruit baskets and breadboards will be blessed. Wherever you go and whatever you do, you will be blessed. The LORD will cause your enemies who rise against you to be defeated before you. They will come at you from one direction but run from you in seven. The LORD will guarantee a blessing on everything you do and will fill your storehouses with grain. The LORD your God will bless you in the land he is giving you. The LORD will establish you as His holy people, as He swore to you on oath, if you keep the commandments of the LORD your God and walk in obedience to Him. And all the people on earth will see that you are called by the name of the LORD, and they will fear you. The LORD will give you prosperity in the land He swore to your ancestors to give you, blessing you with many children, numerous livestock, and abundant crops. The LORD will send rain at the proper time from His rich treasury in the heavens and will bless all the work you do. You will lend too many nations, but you will never need to borrow from them. If you listen to these commands of the LORD your God that I am giving you today, and if you carefully obey them, the LORD will make you the head and not the tail, and you will always be on top and never at the bottom. You must not turn away from any of the commands I am giving you today, nor follow other gods to serve them."

This is all the course of events that was to follow the Hebrews if they were to carefully respect the covenant. Let us continue on to what would happen if they were to violate their end of the agreement. It says in Deuteronomy 28:15-68: "However, if you do not obey the LORD your God and do not carefully follow all of His commands and decrees, I am giving you today, He will put all of these curses on you. You will be cursed in the city and cursed in the country. Your fruit baskets and breadboards will be cursed. Your children and your crops will be cursed. The offspring of your herds and flocks will be cursed. Wherever you go and whatever you do, you will be cursed. The LORD Himself will send on you curses, confusion, and frustration in everything you do, until at last you are destroyed for doing evil and abandoning Me. The LORD will plague you with diseases until He has destroyed you from the land you are entering to occupy. The LORD will strike you with wasting disease, with fever and inflammation, with scorching heat and drought, with blight and mildew, which will plague you until you perish. No rain will fall for you and the ground will be dry and hard beneath you like iron. The LORD will change the rain that falls on your land into powder, and dust will pour down from the sky until you are destroyed. The LORD will cause you to be defeated before your enemies. You will come at them from one direction but run from them in seven, and you will become a horrible sight for all the nations of the world to see. Your corpses will be food for all the scavenging birds and wild animals, and no one will be there to chase them away. The LORD will send boils on you, as He did on the Egyptians. He will make your bodies break out with sores. You will be covered with scabs, and you will itch, but there will be no cure. The LORD will strike you with madness, blindness, and panic. You will grope around in broad daylight like a blind person groping in the darkness, but you will not find your way. You will be oppressed and robbed continually, and no one will come to rescue you. You will be engaged to a woman, but another man will take her and rape her. You will build a house, but you will not live in it. You will plant a vineyard, but you will never enjoy its fruit. Your ox will be butchered before your eyes, but you will not eat a single bite of meat. Your donkey will be taken from you, never to be returned. Your sheep and goats will be given to your enemies, and no one will rescue them. Your sons and daughters will be given to another nation, and you will wear out your eyes watching for them day after day, powerless to help them. A nation that you do not know will eat what your land and labor produce, and you will have nothing but cruel oppression all your days. The tragedy around you will drive you mad. The LORD will afflict your knees and legs with incurable boils, you will be covered from your head to foot. The LORD will exile you and your king to a nation unknown to you and your ancestors. There in exile you will worship gods of wood and stone. You will become an object of horror, ridicule, and mockery among all the nations to which the LORD sends you. You will plant much but harvest little, locust will eat your crops. You will plant vineyards and care for them, but you will not drink the wine or eat the grapes, for worms will destroy the vines. You will have olive trees throughout your land, but you will never use the olive oil, for the fruit will drop before it ripens. You will have sons and daughters but you will not keep them, because they will go into captivity. Swarms of locusts will destroy all of your trees and crops of your land. The foreigners living with you will become stronger and stronger, while you become weaker and weaker. They will lend money to you, but you will not lend to them. They will be the head and you will be the tail. If you refuse to listen to the LORD your God and to obey the commands and decrees He has given you, all these curses will pursue and overtake you until you are destroyed. They will be a sign and a wonder to you and your descendants forever. Because you did not serve the LORD your God with joyfulness and gladness of heart, because of the abundant benefits you have received. You will serve your enemies who the LORD will send against you. You will be left hungry, thirsty, naked, and lacking in everything. The LORD will put an iron yoke on your neck, oppressing you harshly until He has destroyed you. The LORD will bring a distant nation against you from the ends of the earth, and it will swoop down on you like a vulture. It is a nation whose language you do not speak. A fierce and heartless nation that shows no respect for the old and no pity for the young. They will eat the offspring of your livestock and the crops of your land until you are destroyed. They will leave you no grain, new wine, olive oil, calves, or lambs, and you will starve to death. They will attack your cities until all the fortified walls in your land, the walls you trusted to protect you, are knocked down. They will attack all cities throughout your country the LORD your God has given you. Because of the suffering your enemy will inflict on you during the siege, you will eat the flesh of your own sons and daughters, whom the LORD your God has given you. Even the most gentle and sensitive man among you will have no compassion on his own brother or wife he loves or his surviving children. And he will not share the flesh of his children that he is eating, it will be all he has left because of the suffering your enemy will inflict on you during the siege of all your cities. The most tender and delicate woman among you, so delicate she would not so much as touch the ground with her foot, she will be selfish toward the husband she loves and toward her own son or daughter. She will hide from them the after birth and the new baby she delivered, so that she herself can secretly eat them. She will have nothing else to eat during the siege and terrible distress that your enemy will inflict on all your cities. If you do not carefully follow all the words of this law, which are written in this book, and do not respect this glorious and fearful name of the LORD your God, the LORD will send extraordinary afflictions on you and your descendants, harsh and prolonged disasters, and severe and lingering illnesses. He will bring on you all the diseases of Egypt that you were afraid of, they will cling to you. The LORD will also bring on you every kind of sickness and disaster not recorded in this Book of the Law, until you are destroyed. You who were as numerous as the stars in the sky will be left but few in numbers, because you did not obey the LORD your God. Just as it pleased the LORD to make you prosper and increase in number, so it will please him to ruin and destroy you. You will be uprooted from the country you are entering to occupy. Then the LORD will scatter you among all nations, from one end of the earth to the other. There you will worship other gods, gods of wood and stone, which neither you nor your ancestors have known. There among those nations you will find no peace or rest. And the LORD will cause your heart to tremble, your eyesight to fail, and your soul to despair. You will live in constant suspense, filled with fear day and night, never sure of your life. In the morning you will say, if only it were night. And in the evening, you will say, if only it were morning. For you will be terrified by the awful horrors you see around you. The LORD will send you back to Egypt in ships on a journey I said you would never make again. There you will offer yourselves for sale to your enemies as male and female slaves, but no one will buy you."

Isaiah 3:17 states, "The LORD will bring sores on the heads of the women of Zion, the LORD will shave their heads and make their scalps bald." This was the conclusion of the terms.

An ark referred to as the Ark of the Covenant was then built, as depicted on the cover of this book. The ark was a sacred chest covered in pure gold. It housed the Ten Commandments, the book of the laws, agreement and sacred relics such as Aaron's (Hebrew high priest) staff. The ark also served as a communication device between the Hebrews and their God, an unrivaled powerful and highly advanced weapon of mass destruction as well as a physical symbol of God. Only those strictly of the priesthood bloodline (Levi tribe) were allowed to handle the ark of God; it was lethal for anyone else to. This was the Hebrews most holy and sacred relic, so sacred and powerful that Adolf Hitler was obsessed with finding it. Hitler and the Nazis, despite their actions, were highly intelligent and advanced people. They understood that the ark was advanced technology that could aid their cause and confirm their place at the top of the world. Hitler and Nazis archaeologists notoriously searched for the Hebrew ark in Africa in hopes to utilize its power. The ark was ultimately a symbol of the covenant between God and His children. Deuteronomy 29:1 teaches, "These are the terms of the covenant the LORD commanded Moses to make with the children of Israel in the land of Moab, in addition to the covenant He had made with them at Mount Sinai." Moses mad sure that the Hebrews were fully aware of the decision they were about to make. Deuteronomy 29:12: "You are standing here today to enter into the sworn covenant of the LORD your God, which He is making with you today, so that you may enter His oath." After serious thought and consideration, the Hebrews in unison agreed to enter the covenant with God. As stated in Exodus 24:3:

"Then Moses went down to the people and repeated all the LORDS words and laws. All the people answered in one voice, we will do everything the LORD has commanded." Moses wrote everything down and finalized the covenant. Exodus 24:6-8 states, "Moses drain half the blood from these animals into basins. The other half he splashed against the alter. Then he took the book of the covenant and read it to the people. They responded, we will do everything the LORD has said, we will obey. Moses then took the blood and sprinkled it on the people and said, this is the blood of the covenant that the LORD has made in accordance with these words." The covenant was officially made and concluded. The Hebrew people were established as not only God's chosen nation but His sons and daughters on earth. Unfortunately, as time went on, the Hebrews fell short by not staying loyal to their end of the contract. Oath breakers they became, as they violated the sacred covenant with their God. A foolish decision made by the Hebrews, a decision which consequences are still being experienced by their descendants today. What happens to them is truly a tragedy and a heart-breaking horror in every regard.

"We cannot change the past, only recover from it. And perhaps learn from its cruel lessons." Dan Pena

-4-
THE FALL

The Hebrews had made an infelicitous decision that cost them a series of disastrous events, events that will follow them to the four corners of the earth where they would be scattered. They violated a blood covenant with a Being who has inconceivable and ineffable power. They have broken their end of the oath with an Immortal Being who is said to reign Supreme over all creation. The God of the Hebrews was unknown to all other nations, He has not revealed Himself to other people of the earth. His intentions were for the Hebrews to be His children on earth, representing and mirroring His Kingdom. He wanted them to be a beacon in the world, leading all nations to righteousness. He planned to establish a united world government where all nations would come to know who He is. A planet ruled by wisdom, love, peace, and harmony. This beautiful planet was supposed to flourish with eternal life. Like the turritopsisdohrnii jellyfish, the Hebrew people were born to live forever. Immortality is their birthright. However, Adam their great father; lived a little over 900 years before he died. This was the consequence for disobeying God, he brought mortality upon his kind. In this fallen state, his near descendant's lifespan ranged from about 500-900 years old. Here are a few of Adams near descendant's ages as stated in Genesis 5:3-13: "When Adam was 130 years old, he had a son in his own likeness, in his own image; and he named him Seth. After Seth was born, Adam lived another 800 years and had other sons and daughters. Altogether, Adam lived a total of 930 years, and then he died. When Seth was 105 years old, he became the father of Enosh. After the birth of Enosh, Seth lived another 807 years, and he had other sons and daughters. Altogether, Seth lived a total of 912 years, and then he died. When Enosh was 90 years old, he became the father of Kenan. After the birth of Kenan, Enosh lived another 815 years old, and he had other sons and daughters. Altogether, Enosh lived a total of 905 years, and then he died. When Kenan was 70 years old, he fathered Mahalalel. After the birth of Mahalalel, Kenan lived another 840 years, and he had other sons and daughters." You can slowly see how the lifespan of the Hebrews ancestors slowly started to decrease. In their original state, the Hebrews were far more superior than they are now, in comparison to their watered-down deathly state. In today's day and age, black people still age fairly slow compared to everyone else; it's to no surprise that their forefathers aged even slower. Time is a good friend of melanated people who are immortal by nature. One thousand years from now only people of color will remain. This fact is what gave birth to the saying "black don't crack." The Hebrews were a high society, a people of high morals, standards, spirituality, education, technology and mysticism. They were a lawful people who were supposed to be an example for all nations of the earth. Instead they became followers of the men of the world where they were planted. They have fallen from their state of righteousness and became an unlawful and immoral nation, a nation leading other nations to sin. Their actions brought about enemies everywhere they went, a series of curses, calamity, war, slavery, captivity, oppression, division, poverty, famine, ridicule, exile, disease, and death. Some of their early enemies were African ancient nations such as the Canaanites, Ishmaelites, Moabites, Hagarites, Gebalites, Ammonites, Amalek, Philistia, Tyre, Rephiam, Zuzim, Emim, Amorites, Nephilim, and countless more nations outside the borders of Africa. Slavery began with the Hebrews in Egypt where they lived for roughly 430 years. At the end of 430 years, on that very day, all the hosts of the LORD went out from the land of Egypt. Egypt afterwards represented the house of bondage to the Hebrews, a country that symbolized slavery and captivity. It was used as a reference point and an example when the subject of slavery came up. As stated in the previous chapter, the Hebrews entered a covenant with their God after leaving Egypt. Post breaking the agreement with their God, He swore to send them back into Egypt if they broke the covenant, although He did not literally mean the land of Egypt. In other words, He meant that He would send them on a long, tormenting, and disastrous journey back into captivity where they will serve as slaves for 400 years. The God of the Hebrews already foresaw the fall of His children, hence why He foretold the patriarch

Abraham of what would become of his offspring in the future. In the book of Genesis 15:13, it reads: "Then the LORD said to Abram'', 'Know for certain that your descendants will be strangers in a land that is not their own; they will be enslaved and mistreated for 400 years." This was a prophecy to be fulfilled long after they left the land of Egypt.

After the Hebrews became an empire, they offended their God continuously following their violation of the covenant. Starting off as a new nation, they demanded to have a human king rule over them as the other nations, in place of their God King. 1 Samuel 12:12: "When you saw that Nahash the king of the Ammonites came against you, you said to me, 'No, but we must have a king to rule over us,' when the LORD your God was your king." This decision led to calamity and division throughout the royal bloodline and empire. After the Hebrew nation became an empire, they were in constant conflict with many nations, one of them being the Philistines. Possessing superior arms and military organization, the Philistines defeated the Hebrews forces during a time of war and occupied part of their land roughly around 1050 BCE. 1 Samuel 4:9-11 reads, "Fight as never before, be men Philistines. If you do not, we will become the Hebrews slaves just as they have been ours. Stand up like men and fight. So, the Philistines fought desperately, and Israel was defeated again. The slaughter was great, 30,000 Israelite soldiers died that day. The survivors turned and fled to their tents. The ark of God was captured, and Eli's two sons, Hophni and Phinehas, died." The Hebrews suffered defeat many times under the rule of their first king. King Saul disobeyed the God of the Hebrews many times, causing his people severe punishment. 2 Samuel 21:1: "There was a famine during David's reign that lasted for three years, so David asked the LORD about it. And the LORD said, "The famine has come because Saul and his family are guilty of murdering the Gibeonites.""

King David was Israel's next king, and he ruled the region around 1000 BC. Just like all of the Kings of Israel, King David fell short when it came to upholding the laws of their God. During his reign, they were punished by plagues and warfare. 2 Samuel 24:15 says, "So the LORD sent a plaque on Israel from the morning until the appointed time. And there died of the people from Dan to Beersheba 70,000 men."

David had a son named Solomon who succeeded him. King Solomon was said to be the wisest and wealthiest man known to the world. He was also credited with building the first holy temple in Ancient Jerusalem around 931 BC. Many people traveled from all around the world after hearing about King Solomon's wisdom to come and learn many of his teachings. Despite all of his wisdom and great accomplishments, he too, fell short and disobeyed the God of the Hebrews. He allowed his foreign wives, whom he was warned not to marry, to sway him into serving foreign gods. His reign lead to civil war and division. After King Solomon's rule, the empire divided into two kingdoms, Israel being one and Judah the other. Israel (11 combined tribes) ruled in the North and Judah (1 out of the 12 tribes) ruled in the south. From this point on, the Hebrews continued to rapidly fall beneath nation after nation as they quickly headed to the bottom.

Around 722 BCE, the northern kingdom Israel was destroyed by the Assyrians. The population was deported as per Assyrian military policy. They were taken as prisoners of war and scattered. This resulted in what we call today the lost 10 Tribes of Israel. In 1 Chronicles 5:26, it reads, "So the God of Israel stirred up the spirit of Pul king of Assyria, the spirit of Tiglath-pileser king of Assyria, and he took them into exile, namely the Reubenites, the Gadgets, and the half-tribe of Manasseh, and he brought them to Halah, Labor, Hara, and the river Gozan, to this day."

Later on, roughly around 598 BCE, Judah was destroyed by the Babylonians. There in Babylon, the survivors were taken as prisoners of war, held captive and enslaved as stated in the book of 2 Chronicles 36:14-20: "All the leaders of the priests and the people became more and more unfaithful. They follow all the pagan practices of the surrounding nations. And they polluted the temple of the LORD that He had made holy in Jerusalem. The LORD, the God of their ancestors, repeatedly sent His prophets to warn them, for He had compassion on His people and His temple. But they mocked the messengers of God, despising His words and scoffing at His prophets, until the wrath of the LORD rose against His people, and nothing could be done. So the LORD brought the King of Babylon against them. The Babylonians killed Judah's young men, even chasing after them into the temple. They had no pity on the people, killing both young men and young women, the old and the infirm. God handed all of them over to Nebuchadnezzar. He carried to Babylon all the articles from the temple of God, both large and small, and the treasures of the LORD'S temple and the treasures of the king and his officials. They set fire to God's temple and broke down the wall of Jerusalem; they burned all the palaces and destroyed everything of value there. The few who survived were taken as exiles to Babylon, and they became servants to the king and his sons until the kingdom of Persia came to power."

The Persians, following their conquest of the Babylonian empire, allowed the Hebrews to go back to their homeland around 538 BCE. The Persians held the region as part of their empire until it fell to Alexander the Great around 356-323 BCE. After the death of Alexander, the region was held by Ptolemy I, and then the Seleucid Empire until 168 BCE. This was around the time the Hebrews revolted under the leadership of the Maccabees whom established the Hasmonean dynasty. The region was nevertheless taken by the Roman Empire in 63 BCE. The descendants of the tribe of Judah, who are also known as the Jews, were filled with resentment in opposition to foreign occupation. Around this time, Jesus the Christ—who is known as one of the heavenly Sons of God—was born of the tribe of Judah (Jews). The condition of the Hebrews was so severe that Jesus, their great ancestor, had to incarnate into their race from the realm of divinity. His mission was to first redeem the fallen house of Israel and bring salvation to the gentiles (rest of the world), all while sealing the new divine covenant to be made with the Hebrews. His message of truth was to liberate the Hebrews by bringing to remembrance self-knowledge and reuniting them with their Heavenly Father—the One who sent Him to fulfill this imperative assignment. However, the Jews rejected Jesus and conspired against Him. As Jesus became more and more popular and influential, He became a threat to the Jews political leaders, but more repugnant was His threat to the Roman Empire.

This led to the Jews handing Jesus over to Roman authorities which resulted in His death. Crucifixion was a Roman tradition to publicly humiliate and make an example out of a person deemed an enemy of Rome. Prior to the crucifixion of Jesus, He left a prophetic message for His people. He foretold them of near upcoming events that would take place. In the book of Luke 21:20-24, Jesus warns the Hebrews, "And when you see Jerusalem surrounded by armies, then you will know that the time of its destruction has arrived. Then let those who are in Judea flee to the mountains, and let those who are inside the city depart, and those who are out of the country should not return. For this is the time of punishment in fulfillment of all that has been written. How terrible it will be for pregnant women and for nursing mothers in those days. For there will be disaster in the land and great anger against this people. And they will be killed by the sword and sent away as captives to all the nations of the world. And Jerusalem will be overrun by foreign nations until their time comes to an end."

What followed the prophecy and the death of Jesus was the complete destruction and fall of Israel as a people. In an attempt to control their own land, the Hebrews eventually fell to the Romans in 70 AD. For the next several centuries, the land of modern-day Israel was conquered and ruled by various groups. Some of these groups are the Persians, Romans, Greeks, Arabs, Seljuk Turks, Mamelukes, Egyptians, Crusaders, Islamists, and several other nations. The Ottoman Empire ruled Israel and most of the Middle East from 1517-1917. After WW1 ended, the 400-year Ottoman Empire rule ended. In 1918, Israel was under Great Britain's rule. In 1922, the League of Nations approved the Balfour Declaration and the British mandate over Palestine. The British controlled Palestine until Israel became an independent state in 1947, years after WW2. Today, as Jesus said, Israel is occupied by descendants of the Khazar Empire (a foreign heathen nation), a Turkic people who stole the identity of the Hebrews while the true Hebrews were exiled and are currently in captivity. The Khazar people converted to Judaism in the 8th century after Russia destroyed their empire around the 11th century. The United States of America, among other nations, assisted these people in giving them the land of Israel on top of billions of dollars in reparations annually. Despite playing absolutely no role in the holocaust, the United States of America are always eager to aid this nation of so called jew-ish people. These people who wrote the narrative of the holocaust and intentionally excluded all other victims of this tragic event, making the story solely about themselves to receive all of the reparations. The result of this led to benefits, land, money, and power. Moreover, the power they have in America is partially due to the role the so-called jew-ish people played in the Trans-Atlantic Slave Trade. It is also because jew-ish elites control a lot of America's affairs due to them owning the majority of their banks, major corporations, media outlets, Hollywood, the porn industry, and their control over the U.S. Federal Reserve System. However, above all, they have a furtive pact with America. While occupying the land of Israel, the so called jew-ish elite are fully aware that the true inhabitants of the land of Israel and chosen people of God are currently held captive in the Americas. They help America keep this secret through miseducation and television programing in order to ensure the identity of the true Israelites is never revealed. This pact between devils secured land, money, and power for both parties. These people are far from the description and condition that the God of Israel states His people would be in today (divided, poor, oppressed, and lost), proving that the so called jew-ish nation are imposters. Genetic studies were done showing that the European Jewish origins are not of the biblical patriarchs Isaac or Jacob. According to phys.org, DNA analysis of Ashkenazic jews revealed that their maternal line is European. It also found that only three percent of their DNA is ancient. According to the Los Angeles Times, all the Ashkenazi jews alive today can trace their roots to a group of roughly 330 people who lived between 600-800 years ago. Hebrew roots run back a lot further than that, as it is deeply rooted in the borders of Africa. But this is to no surprise. Again, these course of events have already been foretold. It is written in the book of Jeremiah 17:4: "You shall discontinue from your heritage that I gave you. I will enslave you to your enemies in a land that you do not know, for you have kindled My anger, and it will burn forever." The God of the Hebrews warned His children numerous times about what would happen if they disobeyed Him, and Moses made sure to meticulously go over all of the terms of the covenant with them. Yet even after the Hebrews broke the covenant with their God, He still had compassion and showed them mercy. Time after time, when they were exiled and held captive in foreign lands, He forgave them and delivered them back to their homeland. When all hope seemed lost for the Hebrews, He went as far as sending His heavenly Son; an untainted pure Spirit (Jesus), into a polluted world to guide His children out of darkness. In the book of Romans 15:8 it reads: "Remember that Christ came as a servant to the people of Israel to show that God is true to the promises He made to their ancestors." However, the Hebrews had proven to be a hard headed rebellious people. They still continued to turn their backs and abandon Him, serve other gods, and live pagan lifestyles. Judges 2:19: "But when the judge died, the people returned to their corrupt ways, behaving worse than those who had lived before them. They went after other gods, serving and worshiping them. And they refused to give up their evil practices and stubborn ways." Today, the curse of the covenant has not yet expired and is still in full effect. Lessons are still left unlearned. The true Israelites, the chosen people of God, are currently in exile once again. They have been banished from their homeland for over 2000 years to this day. Their book says that they will remain in captivity as prisoners of war until they are no longer a nation, this is what it means to truly be destroyed. In a foreign country they would lose their true identity and become a lost nation while continuously being oppressed. The God of the Hebrews stated that this utter destruction of His people would ironically be a sign for the world, to fear God, and learn from the example He made out of His chosen people.

"Exiled and banished, outcasts where ever they go. They are the result of disobedience, a warning sign for all nations to heed. Restless in the world with no place to call their own, until their Father declares them worthy to return back home."

-5-
THE GREAT MIGRATION

"It is a terrifying thing to fall into the hands of the living God" as a Hebrew apostle once said. Israel has fallen and Jerusalem destroyed under the forces of Rome's great general Gnaeus Pompey Magnus. Many Hebrews were killed in Jerusalem and those alive were taken to Rome as prisoners of war. There, they were made into human torches to be set on fire at night, covered in food to be eaten by dogs alive, fed to lions in the arena, dispersed throughout the empire, crucified, and enslaved. According to Joseph Ben Matthis, a famous historian and scholar at the time, an estimated 1,000,000 Hebrews fled into Africa from the period of Pompey to Julius. Some migrated to Egypt, some to Libya, and others to Ethiopia.

This was a common practice with the Hebrews when they were facing hardship or defeat from their enemies and looking to escape captivity. The Hebrews went into Africa when they fled after the Babylonian assault on their country, to escape persecution. Jeremiah 41:17 reads, "They took them all to the village of Geruth-kimham near Bethlehem, where they prepared to leave for Egypt."

Before the birth of Jesus, many nations religious text foretold of His coming into the world. Herod, a Roman mad king of Judea, heard of the prophecy foretelling the birth of Jesus the Christ. This filled Herod with fear because he took the prophecy as a threat to his throne. His insecurities lead him to kill many innocent children as he sought out this child of prophecy that everyone spoke of. The massacre of countless people was not uncommon for him. Herod's extreme behavior was well known. He was notorious for being an intensely insecure jealous man. In 29 BC, he murdered his wife and his brother-in-law after falsely accusing them of having an affair. In 7 BC, he accused two of his sons, Aristobulus and Alexander, of conspiring to overthrow him. He tortured his female slaves for Intel on any further threats to his throne. In 4 BC he executed another one of his sons, Antipater. Herod was a dangerous man and was on a mission to kill Jesus. He did not hesitate to slaughter his own family members, so it was to no surprise that he would send out a decree to murder all Hebrew male children two years old and younger in Bethlehem. Jesus' parents, after hearing the horrible news, took Jesus, packed up, and immediately readied themselves to leave for Egypt. Matthew 2:13: "After the wise men were gone, an angel of the LORD appeared to Joseph in a dream. 'Get up! Take the child and his mother and escape to Egypt. Stay there until I tell you, for Herod is going to search for the child to kill him.'"

When Jesus' family fled to Egypt there was indeed

already an established Jew community there. This community dates back from the fall of Jerusalem at the hands of the Babylonians. Now you must ask yourself, why did the Hebrews always look to flee deep into Africa above other places when facing a crisis? First, I would like to note that Egypt's original name was Kemet, meaning black land. The original Egyptians were dark skinned people as seen in their hieroglyphs. The story of how the people of the land went from dark skinned people to light skinned people could be understood in the similar story of the Native American massacre in the United States of America. European foreigners invaded their land, killed most of the natives, and raped the survivors. Similar to when black slaves were raped by European slave masters, their light skinned mixed offspring were referred to as mulattos. This is how the colored Dominicans, Puerto Ricans, Cubans, Columbians, Brazilians, etc. were born. It was no different with the Egyptians. Egypt was conquered by the Assyrians around 671 BC, by the Persians around 525 BC, and then the Greeks around 332 BCE. After the defeat of Marc Anthony and Queen Cleopatra VII in 30 BCE, Egypt became a Roman province, hence why you see light skinned Egyptians today.

Ethiopia, another place where many Hebrews fled, means country of burnt faces. A name similar to Sudan, meaning land of the blacks. The Hebrews were familiar with Africa and could easily blend in with the African people being that they were dark skinned people themselves. However, when the Hebrews escaped into Africa, the curse of the covenant followed them. There was no where in the world where they could run or hide to escape what awaited them. Jeremiah 42:15-16 reads, "Then hear the LORD'S message to the remnant of Judah. This is what the LORD of heavens armies, the God of Israel, says; 'If you are determined to go to Egypt and live there, the very war and famine you fear will catch up to you, and you will die there.'" They found absolutely no peace in the heart of Africa. Many Hebrews were killed when foreign nations came and invaded the African countries in which they were hiding, but mainly by the natives. Those who survived came together and submerged. They migrated towards West Africa and inhabited a land that was referred to as the Kingdom of Judah, whose official name was Whydah. On today's maps, the name was changed to Ouidah for obvious reasons that will soon be revealed. Here are a few maps identifying the land of the Hebrews in Africa.

The 1766 French map of Africa shows Negroland (West Coast) as being populated by Jews, according to Edrifsithe. (See map in google images)

Emanuel Bowen was an English cartographer who was renowned for his accurate and precise map making. In his 1747 map of Africa, he depicts the land of the Jews as the Kingdom of Judah on the West Coast of Africa. (See map in google images)

Homann Heirs released a map of Africa in 1743. This map from Germany depicts the land of the Jews as the Kingdom of Judah on the West Coast of Africa. (See map in google images)

Leo Africanus created a map of Africa in 1737. This map from Spain depicts the land of the Jews as the Kingdom of Judah on the West Coast of Africa. (See map in google images)

The 1720 map of Africa depicts the land of the Jews as the Kingdom of Judah on the West Coast of Africa.

(See map in google images)

The 1710 map of Africa depicts the land of the Jews as the Kingdom of Judah on the West Coast of Africa. (See map in google images)

I encourage you to look up these maps online and zoom in so you can see it clearly for yourself. The prisoners of war who became slaves in the Americas were taken from a very specific location in Africa. They were taken from a country established by the Jews who migrated out of Israel. This region where the Hebrews resided became known as the Slave Coast. It is very important to know that the surrounding African nations and the African people were fully aware that the Hebrew people were foreigners. They knew that they shared no kinsmen with them and were not the same people despite being the same color. Similar to how the Chinese man, the Filipino man, the Japanese man, and the Korean man share analogous features but differ in many ways. The same way the Hebrew people were surrounded by enemies while living in Israel (North East Africa), is the same way they were surrounded by enemies while living in West, North, Central, and South Africa. Europeans, Asians, and Arabs invaded Africa to colonize it, strip it of its natural resources—gold, precious metals—and to buy skilled, strong slaves for profit. On all of the maps referenced in this chapter, a description is depicted in different areas in Africa describing what can be found in that particular location. This would help the invaders more quickly find what it is they were coming into Africa to possess. For example, in one particular area, it may say Gold Coast (which is where you can find gold), in another area it would say Ivory Coast (which is where you can find timber, coffee, cocoa, etc.). If you look closely on the maps where the Hebrews lived, you can see that on the country of the Kingdom of Judah, it says Slave Coast. This is where the slaves were captured. One of the many lies taught in schools around the world is that Africans sold their fellow African brothers and sisters into slavery. Mothers sold out daughters, fathers sold out sons, neighbors sold out neighbors, and family sold out family members. One big disgusting lie to camouflage what was really done and to ensconce all of the parties involved. So much energy, money, and resources have been stressed and are still utilized today to cover this part of history up. All to continue on concealing the truth and to upkeep a lie that the world agreed to pass down from generation to generation. A truth that exposes all of the criminals who participated in this gruesome act and a truth that identifies the chosen people of God. Africans conspired with each other and with their colonizers, and enemies came to common ground for one purpose. In fact, without business partnerships between African elites, European traders and commercial agents, the slave trade would have been impossible. According to Thornton and Linda Heywood of Boston University, an estimated 90 percent of those shipped to the New World were enslaved by African rulers. Europeans were unable to easily enter and navigate through the West and Central African borders to capture Hebrew captives and force them onto ships. This was mainly due to yellow fever, severe sun burn, malaria, dysentery, other diseases, hazardous offshore reefs, sandbars, dangerous cross currents and coastal geography. These conditions earned Africa the name "white man's grave." They heavily relied on a network of African rulers and traders to bring Hebrew prisoners of war from various regions to slave castles on the West coast. The African role in the slave trade was well known among many African Americans. Fredrick Douglass stated "The savage chiefs of the western coasts of Africa, who for ages have been accustomed to selling their captives into bondage and pocketing the ready cash for them, will not more readily accept our moral and economical ideas than the slave traders of Maryland and Virginia. We are, therefore, less inclined to go to Africa to work against the slave trade than to stay here to work against it." The Civil Rights Congress of Nigeria wrote to tribal chiefs stating: "We cannot continue to blame the white men, as Africans, particularly the traditional rulers, are not blameless." Other African chiefs stated: "In our own oral tradition, slavery is left out purposefully because Africans are ashamed when we confront slavery. Let's wake up and look at ourselves through our own image." The president ofBenin fell to his knees and begged African Americans for forgiveness for their shameful and abominable role on the slave trade. "We cry for forgiveness and reconciliation. The slave trade is a shame and we do repent for it." Other African officials stated: "The people of Benin have asked me to come here and apologize for the government, for the Benin people and for Africa for what we all know happened. Where our parents were involved in this awful, this terrible, trade." African slaveholders and traders did not think of their slaves as Africans. Instead, they saw cultural and ethnic differences that lead them to view the captives as inferior foreigners. After slavery was abolished in England and in the Western world, Africans Arabs and Asians resisted the abolishment of slavery. Africans were greatly distressed because of the wealth gained from selling slaves and from taxes collected from allowing the passage of slaves through their land. They went on to continue slavery for a century after it was abolished around the world. The African people aided the Europeans, Asians, and Arabs to enslave God's chosen people, the Hebrews. Another woe down and many more woes to come. As Jesus foretold His people, what the Hebrews are about to experience are tribulations far worse than anyone has ever experienced before in the world. They are about to truly experience hell on earth. A catastrophe so severe that the God of the Hebrews said He would have to cut the time of this terrible period short or there would be no survivors left of the Hebrew race. The terrifying remorseless event that was to come was none other than the Trans-Atlantic Slave Trade. Psalm 83:4-5: "'Come'," they say, 'let us destroy them as a nation, so that the name of Israel is not remembered anymore.' With one mind they plot together; they form an alliance against you."

57

"The truth lies in your identity which dwells within you. Know yourself and be set free."

6

THE BLACK SLAVES REVEALED

Deuteronomy 28:45-46 states, "All of these curses will come on you. They will follow you and overtake you until you are destroyed, because you did not obey the LORD your God and keep His commandments and statutes that He gave you. These curses will be a sign and wonder on you and your descendants forever."

Before I begin this chapter, I will like to warn the reader that the information presented is graphic, sickening, and heart breaking. The God of the Hebrews, Jesus Christ, and the prophets foretold of this terrible point in time in which the Hebrews would go through. This prophecy dates way back several thousand years, as stated in the book of Genesis chapter 15:13 by. "Then the LORD said to him, 'Know for certain that for 400 years your descendants will be strangers in a country that is not their own and that they will be enslaved and oppressed there.'".

For roughly 400 years, European countries forced Hebrews, who were captured prisoners of war sold by African leaders, onto slave ships and transported them across the Atlantic Ocean. These people, who were experts in agricultural, architecture, engineering, masonry, geography, herbalism, astronomy, mysticism, and music, were torn away from family members weeping in distress and whom were powerless to lift a hand to help. Like animals they were taken from their country, chained together both hands and feet, with a yoke of iron around their necks, given little room for movement. They then were forced to walk hundreds of miles until they reached the sea on the West African side of the Atlantic Ocean. Here, they stood in excruciating pain, waiting to board the ships that would transport them to the new world.

Children with untreated wounds were left screaming as their cries were ignored. This is where they were stripped of their names, their identity, their language, their land, their culture, their history, their rights as human beings, their spirituality, and most importantly their God. Here marks the destruction of the Hebrews, fulfilling the words of their God. American, Caribbean, and South American plantations awaited their arrival as they boarded the ships. Ships jammed packed with a multitude of slaves chained together, traveling for months under the most inhumane conditions. A journey that only one in six Hebrew slaves would survive. Death and disease were all around them. On the ship, women were having their periods on each other; many gave birth on each other only for the newborn baby to drown in all the vomit and blood accumulated from the Hebrew slaves. There was urine, feces, blood, vomit, and all disgusting human bodily fluids and waste everywhere in which they had to sleep. The stench of dead bodies rotting filled the air. It was poisonous just to breathe down at the bottom of the ships where they were kept. It was so bad that many crew members died of disease contracted by the slaves. Diseases were also spread from rats brought on the ships by the Europeans. The rats were biting the Hebrews, wounds were left untreated becoming infected, and viruses were spread among them. This was all on top of the brutal and inadequate treatment of the slaves that they endured when they arrived to the new world. Countless Hebrew people were killed, tortured, and mutilated when being broken into servitude. Many of them could no longer tolerate the pain and suffering and they felt death was the only sensible option. Suicide was a common occurrence; parents even took the lives of their children. They could not stomach or bear witness to innocent little children going through unimaginable pain, freeing them of this brutality was considered a blessing among a curse. The ocean was filled with dead bodies, more accurately millions of them. So much so, sharks would trail the ships knowing the ships were a good source of food. Here is what was said about the slaves thrown overboard. The Dutch merchant William Bosman wrote in an accurate description of the Coast of Guinea in 1705, "I have sometimes, not without horror, seen the dismal rapaciousness of these animals; four or five of them together shoot to the bottom under the ship to tear the dead corps to pieces, at each bite an arm, a leg, or head is snapped off; and before you can tell twenty have sometimes divided the body amongst them so nicely that not the least particle is left."

Sharks migratory patterns changed during this time because of the slave ships. Although the death toll has drastically been lowered throughout the years, it is now estimated about 2.4 million Hebrew slaves died during transport to the new world. That made up number, even though lowered to take away from the magnitude of the slaughter that took place, still speaks volumes. This was scarily only the beginning of things to come. If this many died on their way to the new world, you can only imagine how many more would die in the belly of the beast.

When the surviving Hebrew slaves exited the ships, they were a horror and wonder to the inhabitants of the new world. They boarded the ships Hebrew slaves, got stripped naked and got off the ships branded "black" prisoners of war. "Black" slaves who lost their identity and would later on become known as Haitians, African Americans, Jamaicans, etc. There were many rebellions and slave revolts from the new prisoners of war, but their oppressors had answers for that. One reason for a lot of the rebellions was due to the captives still having the knowledge of who they were. So the slave masters would strip children from their parents, program and teach them their version of their history. Slave masters would travel to other European countries to seek council on breaking the slaves in mentally. They went on to teach the Hebrew people that they were nothing but slaves born to serve and obey their new masters. Disconnecting them from their roots was crucial for the Europeans, as this process eliminated that fighting spirit the Hebrew warriors had left. They would also take the alpha male or leader figure among the slaves and rape him in front of his people. This would discourage anyone from standing up to the slave masters as well as discredit the alpha male among the Hebrews. Children were used as leverage and hung from trees to inflict fear in the elders. They were programed, brainwashed, and faced with psychological warfare since birth. There were breeding camps where relatives, siblings, young or old slaves were forced to engage in sexual intercourse. This was done with the intentions of breeding stronger more fit slaves to perform harsh labor and for sport. There were institutions such as the "Sugar House" where rebellious slaves were sent. Within the walls of these institutions cruelty and torture were used to elicit cooperation. Things were done to them that only the mind of a devil could think up, the things they were doing to little children fills me with a hatred that I do not want to carry in my heart. Writing about it is as if I'm reliving what my ancestors went through, the visual brings tears to my eyes. A man named Willie Lynch, a slave owner in the West Indies, was invited to the colony of Virginia in 1712 to teach his methods to slave owners. The following is a letter written by Willie Lynch **The Making of a Slave**. "I greet you here on the bank of the James River in the year of our Lord one thousand seven hundred and twelve. First, I shall thank you, the gentlemen of the Colony of Virginia, for bringing me here. I am here to help you solve some of your problems with slaves. Your invitation reached me on my modest plantation in the West Indies, where I have experimented with some of the newest and still the oldest methods for control of slaves. Ancient Rome would envy us if my program is implemented. As our boat sailed south on the James River, named for our illustrious King, whose version of the Bible we cherish, I saw enough to know that your problem is not unique. While Rome used cords of wood as crosses for standing human bodies along its highways in great numbers, you are here using the tree and the rope on occasions. I caught the whiff of a dead slave hanging from a tree, a couple miles back. You are not only losing valuable stock by hangings, you are having uprisings, slaves are running away, your crops are sometimes left in the fields too long for maximum profit, You suffer occasional fires, your animals are killed. Gentlemen, you know what your problems are; I do not need to elaborate. I am not here to enumerate your problems, I am here to introduce you to a method of solving them. In my bag here, I have a foolproof method for controlling your black slaves. I guarantee every one of you that if installed correctly it will control the slaves for at least 300 years. My method is simple. Any member of your family or your overseer can use it. I have outlined a number of differences among the slaves and make the differences bigger. I use fear, distrust and envy for control. These methods have worked on my modest plantation in the West Indies and it will work throughout the South. Take this simple little list of differences and think about them. On top of my list is "age" but it's there only because it starts with an "A." The second is "COLOR" or shade, there is intelligence, size, sex, size of plantations and status on plantations, attitude of owners, whether the slaves live in the valley, on a hill, East, West, North, South, have fine hair, course hair, oris tall or short. Now that you have a list of differences, I shall give you an outline of action, but before that, I shall assure you that distrust is stronger than trust and envy stronger than adulation, respect or admiration. The Black slaves after receiving this indoctrination shall carry on and will become self refueling and self generating for hundreds of years, maybe thousands. Don't forget you must pitch the old black Male vs. the young black Male, and the young black Male against the old black male. You must use the dark skin slaves vs. the light skin slaves, and the light skin slaves vs. the dark skin slaves. You must use the female vs. the male. And the male vs. the female. You must also have you white servants and overseers distrust all Blacks. It is necessary that your slaves trust and depend on us. They must love, respect and trust only us. Gentlemen, these kits are your keys to control. Use them. Have your wives and children use them, never miss an opportunity. If used intensely for one year, the slaves themselves will remain perpetually distrustful of each other. Thank you gentlemen. Lets Make a Slave. It was the interest and business of slave holders to study human nature, and the slave nature in particular, with a view to practical results. I and many of them attained astonishing proficiency in this direction. They had to deal not with earth, wood and stone, but with men and by every regard they had for their own safety and prosperity they needed to know the material on which they were to work. Conscious of the injustice and wrong they were every hour perpetuating and knowing what they themselves would do. Were they the victims of such wrongs? They were constantly looking for the first signs of the dreaded retribution. They watched, therefore with skilled and practiced eyes, and learned to read with great accuracy, the state of mind and heart of the slave, through his sable face. Unusual sobriety, apparent abstractions, sullenness and indifference indeed, any mood out of the common was afforded ground for suspicion and inquiry. Let us make a slave.

What do we need? First of all we need a black nigger man, a pregnant nigger woman and her baby nigger boy. Second, we will use the same basic principle that we use in breaking a horse, combined with some more sustaining factors. What we do with horses is that we break them from one form of life to another that is we reduce them from their natural state in nature. Whereas nature provides them with the natural capacity to take care of their offspring, we break that natural string of independence from them and thereby create a dependency status, so that we may be able to get from them useful production for our business and pleasure Cardinal Principles for making a Negro. For fear that our future Generations may not understand the principles of breaking both of the beast together, the nigger and the horse. We understand that short range planning economics results in periodic economic chaos; so that to avoid turmoil in the economy, it requires us to have breadth and depth in long range comprehensive planning, articulating both skill sharp perceptions. We lay down the following principles for long range comprehensive economic planning. Both horse and niggers is no good to the economy in the wild or natural state. Both must be broken and tied together for orderly production. For orderly future, special and particular attention must be paid to the female and the youngest offspring. Both must be crossbred to produce a variety and division of labor. Both must be taught to respond to a peculiar new language. Psychological and physical instruction of containment must be created for both. We hold the six cardinal principles as truth to be self evident, based upon the following the discourse concerning the economics of breaking and tying the horse and the nigger together, all inclusive of the six principles laid down about. NOTE: Neither principle alone will suffice for good economics. All principles must be employed for orderly good of the nation. Accordingly, both a wild horse and a wild or nature nigger is dangerous even if captured, for they will have the tendency to seek their customary freedom, and in doing so, might kill you in your sleep. You cannot rest. They sleep while you are awake, and are awake while you are asleep. They are dangerous near the family house and it requires too much labor to watch them away from the house. Above all, you cannot get them to work in this natural state. Hence both the horse and the nigger must be broken; that is breaking them from one form of mental life to another. Keep the body take the mind! In other words break the will to resist. Now the breaking process is the same for both the horse and the nigger, only slightly varying in degrees. But as we said before, there is an art in long range economic planning. You must keep your eye and thoughts on the female and the offspring of the horse and the nigger. A brief discourse in offspring development will shed light on the key to sound economic principles. Pay little attention to the generation of original breaking, but concentrate on future generations. Therefore, if you break the female mother, she will break the offspring in its early years of development and when the offspring is old enough to work, she will deliver it up to you, for her normal female protective tendencies will have been lost in the original breaking process. For example take the case of the wild stud horse, a female horse and an already infant horse and compare the breaking process with two captured nigger males in their natural state, a pregnant nigger woman with her infant offspring. Take the stud horse, break him for limited containment. Completely break the female horse until she becomes very gentle, whereas you or anybody can ride her in her comfort. Breed the mare and the stud until you have the desired offspring. Then you can turn the stud to freedom until you need him again. Train the female horse where by she will eat out of your hand, and she will in turn train the infant horse to eat out of your hand also. When it comes to breaking the uncivilized nigger, use the same process, but vary the degree and step up the pressure, so as to do a complete reversal of the mind. Take the meanest and most restless nigger, strip him of his clothes in front of the remaining male niggers, the female, and the nigger infant, tar and feather him, tie each leg to a different horse faced in opposite directions, set him a fire and beat both horses to pull him apart in front of the remaining nigger. The next step is to take a bull whip and beat the remaining nigger male to the point of death, in front of the female and the infant. Don't kill him, but put the fear of God in him, for he can be useful for future breeding. The Breaking Process of the African Woman Take the female and run a series of tests on her to see if she will submit to your desires willingly. Test her in every way, because she is the most important factor for good economics. If she shows any sign of resistance in submitting completely to your will, do not hesitate to use the bull whip on her to extract that last bit of resistance out of her. Take care not to kill her, for in doing so, you spoil good economic. When in complete submission, she will train her off springs in the early years to submit to labor when the become of age. Understanding is the best thing. Therefore, we shall go deeper into this area of the subject matter concerning what we have produced here in this breaking process of the female nigger. We have reversed the relationship in her natural uncivilized state she would have a strong dependency on the uncivilized nigger male, and she would have a limited protective tendency toward her independent male offspring and would raise male off springs to be dependent like her. Nature had provided for this type of balance. We reversed nature by burning and pulling a civilized nigger apart and bull whipping the other to the point of death, all in her presence. By her being left alone, unprotected, with the male image destroyed, the ordeal caused her to move from her psychological dependent state to a frozen independent state. In this frozen psychological state of independence, she will raise her male and female offspring in reversed roles. For fear of the young males life she will psychologically train him to be mentally weak and dependent, but physically strong. Because she has become psychologically independent, she will train her female off springs to be psychological independent. What have you got? You've got the nigger women out front and the nigger man behind and scared. This is a perfect situation of sound sleep and economic. Before the breaking process, we had to be alertly on guard at all times. Now we can sleep soundly, for out of frozen fear his woman stands guard for us. He cannot get past her early slave molding process. He is a good tool, now ready to be tied to the horse at a tender age. By the time a nigger boy reaches the age of sixteen, he is soundly broken in and ready for a long life of sound and efficient work and the reproduction of a unit of good labor force. Continually through the breaking of uncivilized savage nigger, by throwing the nigger female savage into a frozen psychological state of independence, by killing of the protective male image, and by creating a submissive dependent mind of the nigger male slave, we have created an orbiting cycle that turns on its own axis forever, unless a phenomenon occurs and re shifts the position of the male and female slaves. We show what we mean by example. Take the case of the two economic slave units and examine them closely. The Nigger Marriage We breed two nigger males with two nigger females. Then we take the nigger males away from them and keep them moving and working. Say one nigger female bears a nigger female and the other bears a nigger male. Both nigger females being without influence of the nigger male image, frozen with an independent psychology, will raise their offspring into reverse positions. The one with the female offspring will teach her to be like herself, independent and negotiable (we negotiate with her, through her, by her, we negotiate her at will). The one with the nigger male offspring, she being frozen with a subconscious fear for his life, will raise him to be mentally dependent and weak, but physically strong, in other words, body over mind. Now in a few years when these two offspring's become fertile for early reproduction we will mate and breed them and continue the cycle. That is good, sound, and long range comprehensive planning. Warning: Possible Interloping Negatives Earlier we talked about the non economic good of the horse and the nigger in their wild or natural state; we talked out the principle of breaking and tying them together for orderly production. Furthermore, we talked about paying particular attention to the female savage and her offspring for orderly future planning, then more recently we stated that, by reversing the positions of the male and female savages, we created an orbiting cycle that turns on its own axis forever unless a phenomenon occurred and resift and positions of the male and female savages. Our experts warned us about the possibility of this phenomenon occurring, for they say that the mind has a strong drive to correct and recorrect itself over a period of time if I can touch some substantial original historical base, and they advised us that the best way to deal with the phenomenon is to shave off the brute's mental history and create a multiplicity of phenomena of illusions, so that each illusion will twirl in its own orbit, something similar to floating balls in a vacuum. This creation of multiplicity of phenomena of illusions entails the principle of crossbreeding the nigger and the horse as we stated above, the purpose of which is to create a diversified division of labor thereby creating different levels of labor and different values of illusion at each connecting level of labor. The results of which is the severance of the points of original beginnings for each sphere illusion. Since we feel that the subject matter may get more complicated as we proceed in laying down our economic plan concerning the purpose, reason and effect of crossbreeding horses and nigger, we shall lay down the following definition terms for future generations. Orbiting cycle means a thing turning in a given path. Axis means upon which or around which a body turns. Phenomenon means something beyond ordinary conception and inspires awe and wonder. Multiplicity means a great number. Sphere means a globe. Cross breeding a horse means taking a horse and breeding it with an ass and you get a dumb backward ass long headed mule that is not reproductive nor productive by itself. Crossbreeding niggers mean taking so many drops of good white blood and putting them into as many nigger women as possible, varying the drops by the various tone that you want, and then letting them breed with each other until another cycle of color appears as you desire. What this means is this; Put the niggers and the horse in a breeding pot, mix some assess and some good white blood and what do you get? You got a multiplicity of colors of ass backward, unusual niggers, running, tied to a backward ass long headed mule, the one productive of itself, the other sterile. (The one constant, the other dying, we keep the nigger constant for we may replace the mules for another tool) both mule and nigger tied to each other, neither knowing where the other came from and neither productive for itself, nor without each other. Control the Language. Crossbreeding completed, for further severance from their original beginning, we must completely annihilate the mother tongue of both the new nigger and the new mule and institute a new language that involves the new life's work of both. You know language is a peculiar institution. It leads to the heart of a people. The more a foreigner knows about the language of another country the more he is able to move through all levels of that society. Therefore, if the foreigner is an enemy of the country, to the extent that he knows the body of the language, to that extent is the country vulnerable to attack or invasion of a foreign culture. For example, if you take a slave, if you teach him all about your language, he will know all your secrets, and he is then no more a slave, for you can't fool him any longer. For example, if you told a slave that he must perform in getting out "our crops" and he knows the language well, he would know that "our crops" didn't mean "our crops" and the slavery system would break down, for he would relate on the basis of what "our crops" really meant. So you have to be careful in setting up the new language for the slaves would soon be in your house, talking to you "man to man" and that is death to our economic system. In addition, the definitions of words or terms are only a minute part of the process. Values are created and transported by communication through the body of the language. A total society has many interconnected value system. All the values in the society have bridges of language to connect them for orderly working in the society. But for these language bridges, these many value systems would sharply clash and cause internal strife or civil war, the degree of the conflict being determined by the magnitude of the issues or relative opposing strength in whatever form. For example, if you put a slave in a hog pen and train him to live there and incorporate in him to value it as a way of life completely, the biggest problem you would have out of him is that he would worry you about provisions to keep the hog pen clean, or the same hog pen and make a slip and incorporate something in his language whereby he comes to value a house more than he does his hog pen, you got a problem. He will soon be in your house." Countless more horrific things were done to the slaves. Many slaves were whipped to the point that the flesh on their backs was torn off, pepper was rubbed into the wounds to cause more pain. Others were whipped to the point of death. Fathers were forced to bear witness of their wives, sons, and daughters being raped. Sons had to see brothers, uncles, and father's genitals being cut off and shoved into their mouths as a form of punishment. Crying mothers had their babies ripped from their arms, and their young sold to other plantations while the men were powerless to do a thing. Holes were dug in the ground and pregnant women were placed in them as they were beaten. Often times, full term pregnant women bellies were cut open so the baby they were carrying would fall out of their stomachs onto the ground, only to be stomped to death by their oppressors. Women were hoisted up by their thumbs and whipped and slashed with knives before other slaves until they died. Men, pregnant women, and children were tied to posts and burned alive while towns of the new world watched. It was an exciting showing for the Europeans when a lynching or burning was taking place. For them it was like attending a circus. They would bring the community out, both elders and children, to watch as the slaves were hung from trees. A sight they did not want to miss; the bodies of young and old slaves violently shaking, gasping for life as they are being strangled to death. The ones whose neck broke instantly were the lucky ones, they were fortunate enough to not have to fully experience the weight of their bodies being solely supported by their necks. Their rotting bodies were left hanging in the streets for all eyes to see and to serve as warnings. The slaves were slowly and effectively divided, as a consequence they turned against each other. Slave masters would force the slaves to whip each other and take the life of his/her brother or sister. They were forced to fight each other to the death for entertainment, breaking the little unity they had left. The Hebrew captives could not fathom the things the mind of these inhumane, devilish people would conjure up to do to them. Slave masters would skin the slaves alive and make shoes out of the slave's skin.

They would boast about how much the human skin made leather was superior to all other leathers. No one was safe from the harsh treatment or the fatal labor forced upon them. Not elders, pregnant women, young children, or babies. Children suffered extremely high mortality rates. Babies born of slaves were often skinned alive and used as alligator bait. They would bait in alligators for the alligators to be captured and used for various reasons, such as shoes, belts, jackets, leather, zoos, etc. This heinous act practiced in America as well as Europe was also known as "gator bait." It is estimated that half of all enslaved infants died in their first year of life. The number one contribution to this high mortality rate of these babies was chronic malnourishment. Child slave mortality rates reached as high as 90 percent. The average time the slaves worked was 15-16 hours per day, in which pregnant women were not given a break. They still had to perform three-quarters or more the amount of work of women who were not pregnant. The severe labor was one of the numerous ways so many slaves died. Disease was another, due to the slaves being fed low nutrition, which was purely a starch and pork-based diet. Some of the common diseases of the enslaved were abdominal swelling, bowed legs, hypertension, skin lesions, diabetes, blindness, and convulsions. Other common conditions they had were beriberi, pellagra, rickets, tetany, kwashiorkor, diarrhea, dysentery, whooping cough, worms, and respiratory diseases. "Black" people caught all of the diseases the God of their ancestors said they would in Deuteronomy chapter 28. The life expectancy of a slave was 21 years. They were dying left and right, having an immensely high mortality rate. The slaves woke up and went to sleep uncertain if they would live to see another day, as the God of their ancestors said they would be. It is estimated that the total number of deaths during slavery is between 60-100 million people.

There were many rebellions among the slaves, several which were successful. However, no matter how high the slaves would rise, they would always be brought back down. There simply is no way of going around the curse of the covenant or the word of God. A good example of this is the Haitian revolution. The honorable Haitians rose up against their subjugation, most notably in Haiti in the Revolution of 1791-1804. These Hebrew warriors bravely fought three of the world's super powers at the time (Britain, France, and Spain) and won. An event that marked the turning point of the slave trade forever. Their victory has released the chains off of the western hemisphere. Their revolt was so impactful that assistance was requested of the Haitians in the Eastern Hemisphere by many countries. Their victory is arguably responsible for the existence of the United States of America, due to the Louisiana Purchase. The Haitian revolution was the most powerful, influential, and successful slave rebellion in history. Slavery was abolished in the 18th century; this decision was also partially influenced by the Haitian revolution. After becoming one of the first black countries to join the United Nations in 1945, Haiti was established as a symbol of black independence and a proponent for the liberation of Africa from colonial rule. Haiti has paved the way for every African nation to be free today, yet, the African Union denied Haiti membership. This is evidence that the Hebrew people are seen as foreigners to African people, a fact clear to them as night and day.

Unfortunately, despite their extraordinary accomplishments, the sacrifice the Haitians made led them to become one of the poorest countries and one of the most hated ethnic groups of people in the world. Their untold story has freed and spared millions of lives. Sadly, the countries that enslaved the Hebrews and the countries that utilized their assistance to gain independence, turned their backs on them and labeled them devil worshipers. Even today, many Haitians were brainwashed into believing that their own people are evil, and the calamities they face are due to consequences of devil worship. This lie and miseducation was one of the Europeans successful psychological strategies to mentally destroy the Hebrew people. The following prayer is the prayer of Dutty Boukman at the vodou ceremony prior to the Haitian revolution. He was a vodou priest and an early leader of the revolution. "The God who created the earth; who created the sun that gives us light. The God who has ears to hear. You who are hidden in the clouds; who watch us from where you are. You see all that the white man has made us suffer. The white man's god asks him to commit crimes. But the God within us wants us to do good. Our God, who is so good, so just, He orders us to revenge our wrongs. It's He who will direct our arms and bring us the victory. It's He who will assist us. We all should throw away the image of the white man's god who is so pitiless. Listen to the voice of liberty that speaks in all our hearts." Does this prayers sound like a prayer of a devil worshiper or the prayer of a God fearing man? Haiti, also known as the land of high mountains, is a country of heroes, and the story of the Haitians will never be forgotten.

There were many hands involved in the brutalization of the Hebrew people. Some of the participants in the Trans-Atlantic slave trade included Arabs, Berbers, countless African ethnic groups, Italians, Portuguese, Spaniards, Dutch, European Jewish people (Khazars), Germans, Swedes, French, English, Danes, European Americans, Native Americans, and Asians. The Trans-Atlantic slave trade was by far the biggest deportation of all time and a major deterring factor in the world's economy of the 18th century. The fruits of slave labor during the slave trade funded the growth of global empires. France's greatest source of wealth was sugar, also known as white gold, produced by the Haitians in Haiti. More riches flowed in Britain from the slave economy of Jamaica than all of the 13 American colonies combined.

In America, the invention of the cotton gin took the South's national economic wealth and elevated it into a global phenomenon. The slave trade also had a devastating effect on Africa. Economic impetus of African leaders, warlords, and tribes drove their involvement in the atrocity of the slave trade which prompted an atmosphere of violence and lawlessness. African leaders admitted to this. "He knows the damage on our side that came from slaver. He knows how this robbed our own society at home, how it turned us against each other." All of these nations benefitted off of the blood, sweat, tears, and lives of the slaves yet they refuse to pay a penny in reparations or return them back to their country. The so-called jew-ish people who converted to Judaism received reparations as well as the Aleuts, Japanese, 17 Native American tribes, Native Hawaiians, etc. America pays billions of dollars every year to the jew-ish people who owned slaves and persecuted "black people" in the same way the Nazis did. Why can't they pay back "Black people" who were responsible for building America? Why can't they pay back "black people" for defeating the French which led to the formation of the United States of America? The reason being, we are still looked at as their prisoners of war. We are looked at as property that they Europeans still currently own. Everyone is still reaping the benefits of slavery today while the captives continue to suffer its negative effects, as it has always been throughout the story of the Hebrews. Today, major cooperation's profit off the labor of "black people." Profit is made off "black" entertainers, inventions, medicine, etc. Foreigners come to America and establish their businesses in urban neighborhoods knowing the people there will be their number one consumer. "Black people" have the most spending power, spending $1.2 trillion annually. This fact is well known to other nations. Everyone is getting rich off the oppressed while the oppressed remain poor. The world continues to squeeze the life and resources out of them until there is nothing left. Everyone has perpetually profited off everything that has come out of "black people" and everything they are. Studies were done on the lifespan of a dollar in different communities in America. It concluded that in the Asian community the lifespan of a dollar is 28 days, in the jew-ish community, roughly 20 days, in the White community, roughly 17 days, and in the "Black" community, roughly six hours. Villainously enough, after stripping them of their history and human rights, they gained off their labor, replaced their history with a lie, sold and profited off their actual history book (the

Bible). A history book sold all around the world which went on to be the number one selling book of all time.

After slavery ended, the economic success of former slaves during reconstruction led to the birth of the Ku Klux Klan. Although the prisoners of war were degraded and programed to think very little of themselves, they were a great threat. Everyone seems to see the power in "black people" that they do not quite see in themselves. The world mutually keeps Hebrews down because it is the only way to keep them on an equal playing field. Look at what the Hebrews have accomplished while being strategically put at such an immense disadvantage. The world fears that If the Hebrews rise even a little bit, they will become an unstoppable force that would do onto the world what has be done to their people. For this reason, slaves were forbidden to read and it meant death if they were found peeking in a book. This clearly proves that the Europeans were afraid of the slaves gaining knowledge, as it is commonly known that knowledge is power. Today, Hebrews cannot be killed for reading so now they limit the education and provide poor schooling in urban towns. Keeping "black people" uneducated has been a high priority for their oppressors since they were captured. The effects of this programming are still alive today hence the saying, "the best way to hide something from black people is to put it in a book." The Hebrews created thriving communities as soon as 10 years after slavery and had gained political power, such as governorships and Senate seats. There were many of them who became millionaires. The direction towards "black" economic empowerment, in which the Hebrews were rapidly moving, threatened the old economic order. The

Hebrews were given dumps to live in and "hoods", yet they, in turn, built beautiful cities. Black Wall Street was built, airports, schools, thriving businesses, and a strong community. Hebrew individuals and entire Hebrew communities became victims of acts of terror. Europeans bombed black Wall Street, churches, businesses, homes, and much more in hopes to enforce economic poverty. As a community, whenever the "black" captives would build and thrive economically, the Europeans would terrorize them and destroy what they have established, retarding their progress. The Hebrews went from suffering harsh slavery, only to later suffer severe oppression and terrorism. They have faced slave codes, Jim Crow laws, segregation, repeated lynching's, Tulsa race riot, the Birmingham bombing, the Charleston church massacre, Springfield Macedonia fire, Knoxville Inner city Baptist church fire, Louisiana fire of four churches, Manning church fire, Longdale church assault, 1985 Philadelphia bombing by the local police, the Emmett Till massacre, the Will Brown lynching, police brutality—the list goes on and on. All of this without a doubt resulted in the destruction of the Hebrews language, culture, history, spirituality, unity, nation, mental health, self-esteem, self-dignity, self-love, self-worth, and worst of all self-knowledge. Today, the average income of the Hebrews in America is $38,000 in comparison to whites whose average income is six figures. Roughly 6.8 million former slaves are locked up making up more than 40 percent of the prison population and are five times more likely to end up behind bars than whites. Over 65 percent of former slave children grow up in single parent home. "Black people" have to deal with being put in ghettos with liquor stores all around their neighborhoods, miseducation, drugs and guns being planted within their towns, music promoting "black" on "black" violence, police genocide, poverty, gentrification, and mass incarceration. Urban town water supply has been poisoned with high levels of fluoride, lead, and chlorine. Chemtrails are being dumped over their cities and abortion clinics are promoted all around them. There are endless levels of attacks from all areas. Anywhere the Hebrews go in the world they are persecuted, looked down on, and oppressed. This global hatred towards "blacks" prompted the banner of the British Black Panthers reading, "Black oppressed people all over the world are one." Is it not odd that "black people" are terrorized and killed in broad daylight and it's treated as a normal common occurrence? Is it not odd that after being enslaved for 400 years, "black people" face persecution, discrimination, and racism on a global scale? Is it not odd that "black people" have a mutual understanding that they are despised where ever they step foot on the planet? Is it not odd that "black people" have been tagged criminals, thugs, murderers, rapists, thieves, etc. when they are precisely the victims of such labels? Is it not odd that you have been labeled "black"? "Blacks" are hated and mistreated where ever they go and are truly at the bottom of the socioeconomic ladder. The reason being is simple, the so-called "black" prisoners of war are a special nation of people, who are in fact, the direct descendants of the ancient Hebrews that are currently living out the curse of the covenant between their ancestors and their God—a curse aging several thousand years old. Although their history book has been white washed, literally all of these events have been foretold and documented in the Bible. "Negros" share more God like qualities than anyone else on earth. Even though we are mistreated by Africans, Europeans and everyone else on earth, we are still quick to forgive. We would rather hurt each other than our oppressors and murderers. As our Heavenly Father, we are slow to anger and quick to forgive. We do not hate anyone, we are compassionate to our core. The qualities of our Father is in us as described in the book of Psalms chapter 103 verse 8- "The LORD is compassionate and gracious, slow to anger, abounding in love." I believe I speak for my people when I say, all we want is for the truth to be told, to be given what is owed to us, equality and to be left alone. We do not seek revenge, but we desire to stop being harassed, treated unfairly and disrespected.

It is difficult to see the black presence in the Bible today because the language and terminology changed. You won't read terms like African, African American, Haitians, Negros, etc. You will read terms such as Cushite's, Ethiopians, Egyptians, Hamites, Hebrews, or other tribal names. Ethiopia is mentioned about 45 times in the Bible and Egypt about 700 times. Africa as a whole is mentioned more than any other landmass. Remember the "Middle East", including the Holy land, is naturally connected to Africa sharing tectonic plates and was referred to as North East Africa. Due to political geography, it was changed. If the world admits this, they would have to admit their global deceit, and they would have to rewrite everything we know about history today.

Zondervan's Compact Bible Dictionary: Ham —

The youngest son of Noah, born probably about 96 years before the Flood; and one of eight persons to live through the Flood. He became the progenitor of the dark races; not the Negroes, but the Egyptians, Ethiopians, Libyans, and Canaanites.

Song of Solomon 1:5 – "I am black but lovely, O daughters of Jerusalem, dark as the tents of Cedar, dark as the curtains of Solomon's tents."

Job 30:30 – "My skin is black, and my bones are burned with heat."

Revelation 1:14-15 – "The hair on his head was white like wool, as white as snow, and his eyes were like blazing fire. His feet were like fine bronze, as if they burned in a furnace; and His voice as the sound of many waters."

Judges 16:19 – "After putting him to sleep on her lap, she called for someone to shave off the seven locks of his hair. In this way she began to bring him down, and his strength left him."

1 Peter 3:3 – "Do not let your adorning be external such as the braiding of hair, and the putting on of gold jewelry, or the clothing you wear."

"When Pope Pius XII died, Life magazine carried a picture of him in his private study kneeling before a black Christ. What was the source of their information? All white people who have studied history and geography know that Christ was a black man. Only the poor, brainwashed American Negro has been made to believe that Christ was white, to maneuver him into worshipping the white man."

- Malcom X

"Because if Negroes are created in God's image, and Negroes are black, then God must be black, in some sense, be black!" - Marcus Garvey

"Christianity in Africa is so old that it can be rightly described as an indigenous, traditional and African religion." - Dr. John S. Mbiti

"And I've seen the promise land. I may not get there with you. But I want you to know tonight, that we, as a people, will go to the Promised Land." - Martin Luther King Jr.

"I am declaring for the world that they (Jewish people) are not the chosen people of God. I am declaring for the world that you, the black people are." - Louis Farrakhan

"You (Jewish people) will never be able to live here in peace, because you left here black and came back white."- Gamal Abdel Nasser, President of Egypt 1952

Revelation 2:9 – "I know about your suffering and your poverty, but you are rich. I know about the blasphemy of those who say they themselves are Jews, and are not, but are a synagogue of Satan."

Revelation 3:9 – "I will force those who belong to the synagogue of Satan, who claim to be Jews though they are not, but are liars—I will make them come and bow down at your feet. They will acknowledge that you are the ones I love."

We went from being prisoners in Egypt, to being prisoners in Assyria, to being prisoners in Babylon, to being prisoners in Persia, to being prisoners in Greece, to being prisoners in Rome, to being prisoners in Africa, to being prisoners in Europe, to being prisoners in Asia, to being prisoners in Australia, to being prisoners in the Islands of the sea, to being prisoners in Greenland, to currently being prisoners in the Americas. We have been prisoners of the entire world. You can't call yourself free when you were never returned to the land from which you were taken, your home land. You can't call yourself free until you are united with the God who chose your people. We are currently living in the land of the people that conquered us. These are the people who presently rule over us and get away with treating us however they desire, proving that they still hold us captive. However, the book of Ezra 9:9 reads, "Though we are slaves, our God has not abandoned us in our slavery…"

I want to turn the attention of my people to something of grave importance. You who have been labeled as "black people," you who are the bottom of the socioeconomic ladder, who fill the prison cells, who are a divided nation, who have been stripped naked of your identity, who are being kept down by all nations, who are hated all around the world, who are a mockery in all countries, who are currently prisoners of war, and are descendants of the Trans-Atlantic slave trade. You are rich and the most influential group of talented people on this planet. You are the salt of the earth, you who are the ones who bring soul into the world and who are God's chosen people. You are Hebrew! Turn your attention far away from the white versus black drama, black people versus the world drama, oppression, slavery, and racism. Your story is above such petty, small things in the face of the bigger picture. All of these things that have happened to you are tools and instruments used by your God and Father to teach you a valuable lesson. Your oppressors are simply being used by Him to chastise you. Instead of marching, rioting, holding up signs, and complaining, you should be seeking the One who has cursed you and brought all of these horrific events on you and your ancestors. You should be seeking the One who cast your people into slavery, sent all the diseases that are currently killing you, scattered you throughout the world, and exiled you. You need to worry about yourselves and your community, let the God of your ancestors take care of the rest of the world. They will pay for their crimes and the crimes of their forefathers, the same way we had to pay and are currently paying for the crimes of our forefathers. We must unite, learn who we are, claim our true nationality (Hebrew), and build. Here is what God said about you and your ancestors in the book of Isaiah 43:4-6: "Since you are precious and honored in My sight, and because I love you, I will give people in exchange for you, nations in exchange for your life. Do not be afraid, for I am with you. I will bring your children from the east and gather you from the west. I will say to the north, 'Give them up!' and the south, 'Do not hold them back.' Bring My sons from afar and My daughters from the ends of the earth." The One responsible for all of this is the only One who can reverse our situation and the only One who can lift the curse. The strength of all the men in the world can never match the power of the words of God. This is evident in the attempts of all our great fallen leaders. We will never prosper until we root cause our common issue. Your situation is about a God and His people, a Father and His children, it is a story about immortals. Middle ground is not an option for you as it is for everyone else. You are not like the other people of this world as crazy as that may sound. You were holy from the very beginning, meaning set apart. The world is aware of this; however, you are not. You're more valuable than you currently understand. In Hebrews 12:7, it reads: "As you endure this divine discipline, remember that God is treating you as His own children. Who ever heard of a child who is never disciplined by its father?" We are a strong people, which is how we were able to make it through all of these catastrophes and survive. Consequently, our strength has been our down fall. We get complacent and are extremely hard headed. There is nothing but misery and destruction away from our heavenly Father. We were made for one purpose and that is to live in unison with Him always. We are supposed to live by the spirit (our true nature) and not by the flesh (temporary bodies). Your ancestors walked and talked with God, and they were at the top of society. This was before they decided to walk with mankind instead and fell down to the bottom of the barrel. What I am telling you needs to be the utmost priority in your life. This is bigger than your jobs, your hobbies, your family, and your very existence. It is why all of these things are happening to you and has happened to your ancestors. It is why you are still currently being kept down by all nations at all cost. It is why Jesus incarnated into this world to offer up His life for you and your ancestors. You have to come to know who you are, unite with your Hebrew brothers and sisters, and inwardly seek out the God of your forefathers with all of your hearts. The day you do this and tap into who you are as a whole, the planet as you know it will tremble and turn upside down. The space force of the United States of America and of the United Nations will go to war with the army that will enter our atmosphere on your behalf. When this takes place, those at the top will quickly be hurled down to the bottom, and you from the bottom will quickly rise to the top. There, your nation will wear the crown of power and authority. "A lie may take care of the present, but it has no future." This truth is what they ultimately fear and have conspired together to desperately prevent from happening. By the use of distractions, <u>food</u>, **religion**, deception, <u>miseducation</u>, and <u>psychological warfare;</u> they have succeeded so far. Although, their success goes hand and hand with the disobedience of your ancestors. Moreover, this is their utmost priority and it is bigger than their families, hobbies, jobs, and very existence. They are fully aware of a simple truth—your rise marks the end of their rule. The devils terrorizing our planet have been murdering our animals, placing them in captivity (zoos), destroying all the forests for money, contaminating the oceans, polluting the air, poisoning the food, creating diseases, creating weapons that have the power to destroy the planet, murdering indigenous people, colonizing the planet, subjugating everything that moves, spewing hatred, spreading unrighteousness, deceiving the world, and shedding innocent blood from their beginning. They are the ones that have never been at peace with anyone or with themselves, they have never been in harmony or in tune with anything. Know that their time is short. These are the people described in the book of John 8:44: "You are the children of your father the devil, and you love to do the evil things he does. He was a murderer from the beginning. He has always hated the truth, because there is no truth in him. When he lies, he speaks his native language, for he is a liar and the father of lies." The ones unharmonious to the earth will finally be dethroned and come face to face with the God of justice and truth. These are the ones that have mentally imprisoned and programmed us to accept the conditions we are living in by forcing false doctrines onto us such as the doctrine of heaven and hell. They teach heaven and hell are destinations after death, that hope or doom is in the afterlife. This ideology leaves you embracing the suffering that they have created while forever seeking hope solely in the grave. It leaves you helpless and unwilling to make a change here and now. They have created a system of hell on earth for you while their system creates heaven on earth for their nation. We need to reconnect with our roots and understand the doctrine of our ancestors. There is no hell or heaven. Those two words are two opposite extremes. They are both where ever you create and bring them, because they are both inward conditions. Heaven is a state of being, when man is governed by love will he then experience heaven on earth. When man is suffering, he will experience hell on earth. Our oppressors spreading these lies contradict themselves stating that the God of unconditional and everlasting love can run out of love for you. They teach, if you die in your sins and if you are found unworthy, you have reached the limit of God's love. If you reach that point you are cast into a burning dark pit, and immortalized solely so you can suffer incomprehensible torment infinitely for a finite sinful life. These devils not only created a false image of God's true people, but they blaspheme God's character and create a false image of Him as well. This doctrine was wickedly thought up in hope to inflict fear so that you comply and never question their false doctrine or agenda. These psychological strategies have made us passive to all of their devilish deeds, imprisoned our minds, and emptied our pockets. The level of crimes they have committed is insanely out of this world. Their end will correspond exactly with their actions and with what they deserve. When that joyous day comes beautiful mother earth as we know her, and all of her native inhabitants will know peace, love, and harmony again. Your rule will bring all of these things about and your self-knowledge will maintain it. Your fear and respect for your God will warranty it. This utopia along with your reign begins at the closing of this Dark Age, and the dawning of the Golden Age. You are literally the sons and daughters of the living God. As it was in the beginning, so it will be in the end. It has already been written, therefore without fail, it will most certainly be done.

"We are not from Africa; we are from everywhere. There is not a place in the world where we haven't left our mark. The keys of the Earth were given to us and we will carry them once again."

7

THE RISE OF THE GOLDEN AGE

Jeremiah 23:3 reads, "Then I Myself will gather the rest of My people out of all the countries where I have banished them. I will bring them back to their country, and they will grow into a mighty nation."

Many have said, in regard to our situation: "It is what it is." As well as: "Sometimes you just have to bite the bullet." I say we have been biting bullets from day one, and if we continue to do so we will be left without any teeth. In fact, we have already become a toothless nation that has lost our way. Now is the time to take this crisis seriously and take action. We need to unite and start rebuilding ourselves, each other and our community. This is only possible through segregation. This may all seem absurd and completely unbelievable to the reader, but so does your unexplainable situation. Think about how inconceivable the things are that your ancestors went through and the unimaginable things that you are still currently going through. If your preposterous situation is this unordinary and hard to digest, it would only make sense that the astonishing unique background of your story is naturally out of this world. Here is the summary of our story. The God of our ancestors decided to have children on earth, whom He elected to be His holy nation, a nation separated from everyone else. He did not choose Africans, Native Americans, Indians, Asians, Hispanics, Latinos or Europeans; but the so-called Negros. Our ancestors broke a sacred covenant with Him resulting in them being cursed and exiled out of their country. Ever since, our ancestors went through a long period of slavery, captivity, oppression and tribulations. The curse of the covenant is a generational curse that is still in effect today and has been passed down for thousands of years. This explains why we (their descendants) went and are currently going through the same exact course of events. Our severe punishment is meant to serve as a valuable and highly necessary lesson. Not just to us but to the entire world. A lesson that teaches that wisdom is to fear God and understanding is to stay away from wrong doing. During our banishment God has called out and extended His love, mercy and promises to the rest of the world. When the period of this great call expires, along with the curse that resides over our people; the Savior will return back to earth. He will gather our people out of captivity, out of all the foreign countries where we currently reside, and restore us to our original state. The world will come together and go to war with the army of our God and utterly lose. We will be brought back to our homeland where we will rule as He intended for us to. The Sprits of God which is us, will finally wake up and we will live accordingly. The lives of our people are the main story line in God's great book of life.

To my Hebrew people, I want you to know that your story has not yet ended. Your story ends with you singing a new song in your home country. Not like the songs of old that we and our ancestors would sing in foreign countries, which are songs of oppression and slavery. We will sing songs of freedom and prosperity. The time period in the Bible that spoke of our exile, enslavement, oppression, tribulations, and destruction, are the dark ages our people are currently living in. It is an important time period that marks the closing of the current age and the expiration of the curse of the covenant. The reign of the gentiles allowed by our God is almost up. All of the back to back disasters, war, immorality, unexplained phenomena, UFO sightings, disease outbreaks, visions, and wide spread enlightenment are all signs of the great shift that is about to take place. World War III is going to be a world war like no other war in the history of the planet, we will be the grand finale and the main event in the closing of this age. Our story did not cease with the death of our great ancestor Jesus Christ or with our destruction. On the contrary, the coming of Jesus went hand and hand with the making of a new divine covenant with the Hebrews. Not a carnal covenant like the old one made with our ancestors, but a divine one sealed by His resurrection from the dead. All sacred covenants demand blood to seal the contract and make the agreement alive, sacrifice is always necessary. Jesus foreknew He would be put to death for preaching the truth and empowering His people. In the same way, some of our honorable leaders like Martin Luther King Jr and Malcom X were killed for empowering us. Jesus knew He would die with one hundred percent certainty and therefore took His death as an opportunity to cover the sacrificial aspect of the new covenant. He therefore willingly gave up His life for us furthermore becoming known as the Lamb of God. Moreover, our ancestors knew and understood that we never truly die, but transition. Our true Self, our Spirit is immortal although the bodies that we live in are mortal. The old covenant with the House of Jacob was temporary, as it pertained to the flesh. Moreover, the new covenant with us is everlasting, as it pertains to our Spirit. Jeremiah 31:33: "This is the new covenant I will make with the people of Israel after those days," says the LORD. "I will put my law in their minds and write it on their hearts. I will be their God, and they will be my people."

Today, we are still in the trials and tribulations phase. We are quickly approaching the phase of revelation. Revelations is the period of enlightenment. This is when the truth will start to rapidly surface from everywhere that it has been buried, and all lies will be exposed in the light of the true Sons of God. After reading and understanding these things, the Spirit of truth will ignite a fire within you, it will spread like wild fire and not be extinguished. Your eye will be opened as mine were. Though you may run from the truth prolonging your suffering, you will not be able to deny it. No matter how far you run and hide, the voice of truth within you will call out to you, whispering, "Know thyself."

I, myself, tried to run away from this truth. I have denied everything I have said to you in this book. I was comfortable with the lies that we have been taught. We have been oppressed and kept down for so long that imagining myself a son of God, in a place of power, and at the top of the socio ladder was unusual and uncomfortable. But I tell you this, you are far more important than you can comprehend at the moment. Jesus was sent by our heavenly Father specifically to remind us of who we are. Matthew 15:24 reads, "Jesus said, I was sent only to help God's lost sheep - the people of Israel." And in Matthew 15:25-26 reads: "The woman came and knelt down before him, saying, 'Lord, help me.' Jesus responded. 'It is not right to take food from the children and toss it to dogs.'" He ended up helping the woman proving that many gentiles will be blessed because of the Hebrews. However, He came to show us the way back to unity with the Spirit of spirits, as all of our prophets and leaders did. "Know thyself and the truth will set you free." Do not worry about other countries or nations, the God of our ancestors will deal with them in due time. The world is in constant fear of us, they fear that the oppressed people with a non-violent history seek revenge. However, they truly should be terrified of the fearsome God of justice. If God can deal this harshly with us, whom He has called His very children, how much more severely do you think He will deal with the nations who harmed and hated His chosen people? The book of Joel 3:2 reads: "I will gather all nations and bring them down to the Valley of Judgement. There I will judge them for harming My people, My special possession, whom they have scattered in foreign countries and divided up My land." Vengeance belongs to the LORD. Isaiah 60:14-16 reads: "The descendants of your oppressors will come bowing before you; all who despise you will bow down at your feet and will call you the City of the LORD, Zion of the Holy One of Israel. Although you have been despised and hated, with no one traveling through, I will make you the everlasting pride and the joy of all the generations. Powerful kings and mighty nations will satisfy your every need, as though you were a child nursing at the breast of a queen. You will know at last that I, the LORD, am your Savior and your Redeemer, the Mighty One of Israel."

In this new world in which we will rule, we will know only life, peace, love, power, prosperity, unity, harmony, righteousness, wealth, and glory. Death, violence, hatred, division, immorality, corruption, poverty, disease, lawlessness, and destruction will be foreign in our land. Our land will be fertile, adorned with gold and precious metals. The economy will thrive and nations will borrow from us, but we will never need to borrow from anyone else. Poverty will be unheard of in our land. Our architecture will be beautiful for the eyes to behold, our engineering superb. Our cities will mirror the heavens and line up with the stars home to our God, its beauty will be rivaled by no other nation on earth. No one will be sick in our country; our food will heal all illnesses. Many nations will come to learn in our schools; the education system will be exceptional. The technology we will develop will be advanced and superior to all others. Our children will dance in the street and eat in our neighbor's home. No one's home will require doors or locks, there will be no need for these things. Love will be found throughout our country's borders, filled in every person and in every living thing. There won't be a need to worry, stress, or have anxiety about a single thing; not a blade of grass will be subject to harm or danger. The music and art that we will create will surpass that of the highest order of angels. We will be lacking in nothing and never be in need. We will be successful in all of our ways. We will be blessed, everything we touch will be blessed and all those who bless us will be blessed. During those days "the wolf will live with the lamb, the leopard will lie with the goat, the calf and the lion and the yearling together, and a little child will lead them all. The cow will eat with the bear, their young will lie down together, and the lion will eat straw like the ox. Infants will play near cobra's dens, and the young children will put their hands into the nest of vipers. Nothing will hurt or destroy in all my holy mountain, as the waters fill the sea, so the earth will be filled with people who know the LORD" says the God of our forefathers. When we are gathered out of America, the Islands and everywhere else we were scattered, many foreigners will join us as they did when our ancestors were delivered out of Egypt. Isaiah 14:1-3: "The LORD will have compassion on Jacob; once again He will choose Israel and will settle them in their own country. Foreigners will join them and unite with the descendants of Jacob. The nations of the world will help the people of Israel to return, and those who come to live in the LORD'S land will serve them. Those who captured Israel will themselves be captured, and Israel will rule over its enemies. On that day the LORD gives His people rest from pain and torment, from slavery and chains."

My Hebrew brothers and sisters, I strongly encourage you to come to know who you are and embrace your true heritage. Let us unite and build our communities, sell to others but only buy from each other. Keep the dollar within the community. We have to become self-reliant and self-sustained. We have to get to the point where we can depend on ourselves rather than other people. Let us build each other up and lay our lives on the line for each other, not die anymore at the hands of one another. Let us put our differences aside and walk together in the name of love and harmony as we build and await our God to deliver us to the land promised to us. We must educate ourselves, our children and support each other. We must also segregate our community as our God intended for us to. We are already somewhat separated, just take a look at suburbs and urban towns. I am more so speaking of the segregation of religion, culture, education, food etc. Segregation will prevent us from the influence of the gods, religion, culture, diet and lifestyles of other nations. We can still communicate and work together with everyone, but we must not subject ourselves anymore to the ways of the world. This is precisely what got our ancestors into the mess we are in today. Deuteronomy 32:7-9 reads: "Think about past generations. Ask your father, and he will tell you, your elders, and they will teach you. When the Most High assigned lands to the nations, when He separated the sons of Adam, He set borders of the peoples according to the number of the children of Israel. For the people of Israel belong to the LORD; Jacob is His special possession." We were a people separated from the very beginning, holy by nature. We are currently divided and we are on different pages, but it is not until we all lift our voices to our heavenly Father in unity will we be heard. This is not an individual journey but a nation's journey, the innocent among us were also cast into slavery for the crimes of our ancestors who violated the covenant. We are a powerful people with soul and our unity vibrates through space and time, on a frequency reaching into the very heart of the Creator. The strength of our people is described in the book of 2 Corinthians 4:8-9: "We often suffer, but we are never crushed. Even when we do not know what to do, we never give up. We are persecuted, but never abandoned by God. We get knocked down, but we are not destroyed." Our story is a unique one that is truly out of this world. We have to exercise faith simply to believe it, even with visible evidence right in front of our eyes. I understand that this is a lot to take in and it is hard to believe that we are much more than we ever believed ourselves to be. It is because we have been lied to, programmed and brainwashed along with the rest of the world. 1 John 5:19: "We know that we are children of God, and the whole world is under the control of the evil one." The evil one is the forefathers of the race of people in power who have been terrorizing the planet in the name of Christianity and Judaism, the ones who are anti-life and anti-Christ. The ones who from the very beginning have done nothing but murder, steal, and lie. The ones who have committed the most inhumane crimes while portraying themselves as the heroes and civilizers of the world. The ones who have shed more blood than all other nation's combined. The ones who are accusers that play victim of crimes they are guilty of. Our history book identifies and warned us of such people in the book of 2 Corinthians 11:13-15: "These people are false apostles. They are deceitful workers who disguise themselves as apostles of Christ. And no wonder, Satan disguises himself as an angel of light. So, it is no surprise if his servants, also, disguise themselves as servants of righteousness. Their end will correspond to their wicked deeds."

When our history book mentions the devil, it is not speaking of a red being with a pitch fork, it is describing a person/people. I do want to note that there is no race of all righteous or evil people. However, a tree is known by its fruit. Immortality is our birth right; we were created in the image and likeness of our Father, the God of Israel. We prolong our mortality and human experience. But I tell you liberation awaits us and is guaranteed, it has already been written. We are destined to move onward. Though the progression may be slow, the end result is absolute. Freedom lies in the knowledge of ourselves where our Father, the Creator and All in all dwells. Lastly, I want to say endure and hold on for just a little bit longer. The hardship we face is almost over. The period of oppression is coming to an end. The time of our second exodus is quickly approaching as well as the new song we will sing. What follows is the dawning of the Golden Age. As our ancestors did, we too, will talk, walk side by side, and live eternally with our God.

Revelation 21:3-4: "And I heard a loud voice from the throne saying, 'Look, God's home is now among His people. He will live with them, and they will be His people. God Himself will be with them, and be their God. He will wipe every tear from their eyes. There will be no more death or sorrow or crying or pain, for the old order of things has passed away.'"

I welcome all to read this book. However, this book is dedicated solely to my people, the house of Jacob; the ones taken as prisoners of war and enslaved. Huey P Newton, Frederick Douglass, Martin Luther King Jr, Malcom X, Marcus Garvey, Louis Farrakhan, Harriet Tubman, Rosa Parks, Muhammad Ali, Lauryn Hill, Bob Marley, Samuel Cook, Colin Kaepernick, Jesse

Williams, the Hebrew prophets of old, the Hebrew apostles, the Hebrew disciples of Christ, the Master Jesus Christ, and all of the other Hebrew leaders that I did not name were all sent to the Hebrews. I say sent because none of them put forth their efforts or put their lives on the line for their own accord or personal gain. We do it because it is right, because of the driving force within us, for the sake and love for our people. That driving force is our heavenly Father who dwells in a higher dimension deep within our hearts, the One who loves us with an everlasting love. Not an emotional love like our tainted definition of what we perceive love to be, but the all-powerful force of real love that has the energy to fill all universes and space with infinite life forms. A love that knows only wisdom and truth. Romans 8:38-39 reads: "For I am convinced that neither death nor life, neither angels nor demons, neither the present nor the future, nor any powers, neither height nor depth, nor anything else in all of creation, will be able to separate us from the love of God that is revealed in Jesus Christ our Lord."

I will now conclude by reminding you of this simple message of truth, come to know yourself in order to come to know your God. I cannot stress it enough. Take this time to really do some soul searching. Self-reflect, love, and respect yourself. Your body is a temple that houses a holy Spirit. The holy Spirit is you. Your superior melanated bodies energized by the sun, is evidence that it is temporarily home to a god. Before you can love your brothers and sisters, you have to first love yourself with an unconditional and everlasting love. Treat yourself as someone you truly need to learn, observe yourself, meditate, and spend time within you. Reconnect with your roots so that you can rise from your sleep and walk in the direction your people are destined to arrive. Stop being who the world portrays you to be. Stop living up to the stereotypes and negative images branded on you. Stop living a lie. Become in tune with your true self, know that you are a god and live accordingly. Do this and you will see yourself as well as your people in an entirely different light. If you are searching for God, stop looking outside of yourself, indulging in all of these misleading religions and doctrines. Go right to the source which is inside of your temple. Your pure and holy Spirit is covered up by ego, masks, and false images. When you finally come to know yourself, all of the coverings will be removed and you will see God face to face. Wake up and fight hard every day to remain awake. We are currently a confused, lost nation of many nations. What I mean by that is we are severely divided. Because of our history of captivity and integration, we have picked up the lifestyles and habits of nations all around the world. Some of us are a part of the Nation of Islam, Kemetism, Christianity, Catholicism, the Nuwaubian Nation of Moors, Five-Percent Nation, Freemasonry, etc. That has been the case for us for quite some time. From Martin Luther King Jr and Malcom X, to the entertainers Biggie Smalls and Tupac. We have had great leaders fighting for a cause separate from their brother's cause. We have had powerful movements turn against each other, such as the original Bloods and Crips. Divided we fall and will never be successful. United we will stand when you accept that you are not meant to be a part of these nations, groups, organizations, or religions. Take a good look at yourself in the mirror and accept that you are Hebrew, a bloodline member of God's chosen nation. If you find yourself back asleep and your identity lost once again, look to your history book and remember who Adam is. Remember who your ancestors are; remember who you are. According to the universal law of attraction, your heart is where your treasure is and you will be given what you truly seek. Although you are harmonious with this planet, you are not of this world. You are alien to it. Your ultimate purpose is to escape the cycle of rebirth by living in truth, resulting in you at last being born into an immortal body; a subject I will go into further detail in future books. If what I am saying to you sits well with your soul and your heart embraces this message of truth, stop referring to yourself and your people as "black people." The original definition of the word "black" before it was changed, means the absence of color. "Black" stands for the negative pole of being and all negativity. On the contrary, "white" means a harmonious blending of all colors. "White" stands for pure spirit and positivity. Judging based off of physical color, actions, history and origin; "black people" should be referred to as "white people" and "white people" should be referred to as "black people" by definition. Every time you call yourself or your people "black", you are calling yourself and your people negative. You are speaking negativity onto yourself and one another. There is great power in words, and what you are doing is ignorantly casting spells on each other by an elementary use of black magic. Accept who you are and refer to yourselves and your brothers and sisters as Hebrews or people of color. I will reference one more chapter in our history book that you can always go back to in remembrance of who you are, a chapter that traces back your genealogy to the roots of our family tree.

Luke 3:23 -28: "Now Jesus Himself was about thirty years old when He began His ministry. He was the son of Joseph, who was the son of Heli, the son of Matthew, the son of Levi, the son of Melki, the son of Jannai, the son of Joseph, the son of Mattathias, the son of Amos, the son of Nahum, the son of Esli, the son of Naggai, the son of Maath, the son of Mattathias, the son of Semein, the son of Josek, the son of Joda, the son of Joanan, the son of Rhesa, the son of Zerubbabel, the son of Shealtiel, the son of Neri, the son of Melki, the son of Addi, the son of Cosam, the son of Elmadam, the son of Er, the son of Joshua, the son of Eliezer, the son of Jorim, the son of Matthew, the son of Levi, the son of Simeon, the son of Judah, the son of Joseph, the son of Jonam, the son of Eliakim, the son of Melea, the son of Men, the son of Mattatha, the son of Nathan, the son of David, the son of Jesse, the son of Obed, the son of Boaz, the son of Salmon, the son of Nahshon, the son of Amminadab, the son of Ram, the son of Hezron, the son of Perez, the son of Judah, the son of Jacob, the son of Isaac, the son of Abraham, the son of Terah, the son of Nahor, the son of Serug, the son of Res, the son of Peleg, the son of Eber, the son of Shelah, the son of Cainan, the son of Arphaxad, the son of Shem, the son of Noah, the son of Lamech, the son of Methuselah, the son of Enoch, the son of Jared, the son of Mahalalel, the son of Kenan, the son of Enoch, the son of Seth, the son of Adam, who is the son of God."

We are gods that have grown comfortable in our shackles. We have lost our way and have been disconnected from our roots. Let us liberate ourselves with self-knowledge, which is the key to our chains. Though they may take away our identity, our history and our land; they can never take away what is hidden deep within us!

THE DESTRUCTION OF ISRAEL
ARCTIC OCEAN
PACIFIC OCEAN
ASIA
AUSTRALIA
INDIAN OCEAN
ISRAEL
EUROPE
AFRICA
GREENLAND
ATLANTIC OCEAN
SOUTH AMERICA
NORTH AMERICA
SOUTHERN OCEAN
ANTARCTICA
ARCTIC OCEAN
PACIFIC OCEAN

Ezekiel chapter 11 verse 17: "This is what the LORD God says: 'I will gather you back from the peoples and assemble you out of the countries where you have been scattered, and I will give you back the country of Israel."

www.ingramcontent.com/pod-product-compliance
Lightning Source LLC
Chambersburg PA
CBHW022157150726
47992CB00002B/829